THE
CASTLE
AND THE
SANDBOX

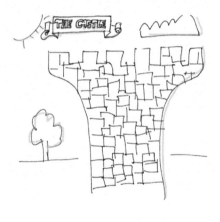

Copyright © Kosta Peric 2012

The author reserves the right to object to derogatory treatment of the work. The author has asserted his moral right to be identified as the author of this book in accordance with Section 77 of the Copyright, Designs and Patents Act 1988.

All rights reserved under international and pan-American copyright conventions.

The contents of this publication, either in whole or in part, may not be reproduced, stored in a data retrieval system or transmitted in any form or by any means, electronic, mechanical, photocopying, recording or otherwise without the written permission of the copyright owner and publishers. Action will be taken against companies or individual persons who ignore this warning. The information set forth herein has been obtained from sources which we believe to be reliable, but is not guaranteed. The publication is provided with the understanding that the author and publisher shall have no liability for errors, inaccuracies or omissions of this publication and, by this publication, the author and publisher are not engaged in rendering consulting advice or other professional advice to the recipient with regard to any specific matter. In the event that consulting or other expert assistance is required with regard to any specific matter, the services of qualified professionals should be sought.

ISBN: 978-1-907720-70-3

Typeset and designed by Deirdré Gyenes

Illustrations by Konstantin (Kosta) Peric

THE
CASTLE
AND THE
SANDBOX
TRANSFORMING CONSERVATIVE COMPANIES IN ESTABLISHED INDUSTRIES USING OPEN INNOVATION

By Kosta Peric

About the author

KOSTA PERIC is a technologist, riding at the point of fusion between technology, finance and innovation. Since 2008, he has been head of innovation at SWIFT and co-founder of Innotribe, the financial industry initiative to enable collaborative innovation.

Previously he was the chief architect of SWIFTNet, the worldwide secure network currently connecting 8,000 banks and 1,000 corporations.

In addition to innovation, Kosta's interests include technology subjects such as the digital asset grid, mobile payments, Big Data, augmented reality, hard AI; and softer topics such as banks for a better world, connecting the unbanked, virtual currencies and new economies.

Kosta contributes columns and articles for Forbes.com, American Banker and other fin-tech publications.

He likes applying his knowledge and experience to support social entrepreneurship.

About Searching Finance

Searching Finance publishes and curates economics, finance and politics.
Follow us on Facebook at www.facebook.com/searchingfinance
Our website is: www.searchingfinance.com

For Lazaro Campos, a friend and a leader, who put all of this in motion. Forward!

For Pascale, who supported and advised me through the ups and downs. With love.

Praise for Innotribe

"Innotribe is all about breaking the mould, about bringing innovation right into the heart of one of the world's most conservative, risk averse financial services organisations. It is also revolutionising how member banks collaborate, in this case through SWIFT. Innotribe has accelerated the incubation and development of innovative ideas that normally would not have seen the light of day. In this sense, Innotribe is truly transformational."

NEAL LIVINGSTON, head of EMEA, Global Transaction Services (GTS), RBS

"I am thankful that Innotribe has succeeded in convincing so many in the financial services industry that, while we compete in our everyday business, we can survive and prosper only through collaborating on innovation."

MIRCEA MIHAEASCU, Director, Technology Research Center, Sberbank

"It was absolutely about the freedom of thinking, the borderless approaches that were discussed and I did not expect this to happen within financial services industries, which I regard as being absolutely old-school. [...] people are openly discussing and exchanging their views on very 'hot issues', like last time talking about alternative currencies. I am sure, you are the only real "think tank" that is that progressive within the financial services industry."

MATTHIAS KRÖNER, CEO, Fidorbank

"Innotribe arrived like a small viral spacecraft into the SWIFT community. It was alien, spread rapidly and created a new species called creators. The mixture of tradition and creativity has led to new worlds being formed and that is why the Innotribe thrives, grows and gains momentum every day."

CHRIS SKINNER, chairman of The Financial Services Club, Owner at Balatro Ltd

"Many innovation centres around the world give lip service to innovation, but they really don't want it. They would rather defend the status quo. With Innotribe, SWIFT has created a genuine innovation hub that eagerly and inventively attracts the best new ideas in banking, finance, currencies and more. Read this book to understand the future of money and value."

JERRY MICHALSKI, founder of The REXpedition

"The story of Innotribe is a story of excitement, progress and most of all – financial innovation! While the world pleads for change in the finance industry, it is heartening to see SWIFT standing up and creating space for progress. It is not just new ways of thinking, but entire new models of exchange that are born as a result."

STAN STALNAKER, Founding Director, HubCulture.com and the Ven currency

Some music for the journey

While you read this story I would suggest the following music as an accompaniment.

- Daft Punk: the "Tron" movie soundtrack
- Parov Stelar: "Coco Pt. 2" album
- Waldeck: the "Ballroom Stories" album
- Praga Khan, the "Twenty First Century Skin" album
- Shantel: the "Disko Partizani" album
- Buscemi: the "In situ" album
- The soundtrack to the movie "Drive"

These albums represent a good sample of the music played at numerous events and which, in my mind, irresistibly make me think of my fabulous team.

CONTENTS

ACKNOWLEDGEMENTS

I'D LIKE TO recognise the following people at SWIFT (or close by) who helped my innovation team and me.

Gottfried Leibbrandt, my boss throughout the innovation years, for recognising us, then walking with us and then running with us.

Francis Van Bever, CFO and member of the Innovation Steering, for challenging and guiding.

The Executive Committee of SWIFT, for supporting the innovation "sandbox".

Christian Sarafidis and Eileen Dignen, for their unrelenting faith.

Isabelle Vanpeteghem, always ready to help.

Contributors to the team: Heather Schlegel (aka Heather-vescent), Jenna Loubris, Cathal Fitzgerald.

Cognito extended communications team, who opened horizons.

Denis Vermeulen, the HR guy who made things happen.

Innovation promoters – "How could drops of water know themselves to be a river? Yet the river flows on." (Antoine de Saint-Exupéry)

The early "black ops team": Brigitte Dewilde, Victor Abbeloos, Tony Martin, Keith Vallance.

The three Megaphones teams, who pushed and continue pushing hard.

And, finally, to colleagues who have become friends over the years – you know when to pop in and re-boost me.

The team
Mariela Atanassova, Peter Vander Auwera and Matteo Rizzi who are co-founders, with me, of Innotribe.

Muriel Dewingaerden, Martine De Weirdt, Greet Michiels, Dominik Debuyser, Karen Declerck and Nektarios Liolios.

I have been asked many times – how does it feel to be the manager of such a team? I often answer that I feel more like the impresario of a rock band.

Some years ago, there was a regular competition organised in a club in Brussels called "Le Mirano".

The competition was dubbed the "Impro-session" and it was about which band could best improvise a song. The typical session would feature two bands, from which the public would select the winner by applause. There were several set exercises in a session, but the most simple was one where the bandleader would ask someone from the public for a song title and a song genre (from opera to rock to rap to ... whatever the person fancied). The band would then have 60 seconds to talk, before starting the improvised song. The song's minimum duration was 3 minutes. One particular band, called "Les extincteurs" regularly won over several years. I was fascinated by how they worked. It was enough for them to look at each other, to make a small gesture to align and move the song to a different tune and chapter. For me, this is the ultimate team dynamic.

In many ways, the Innotribe team is like that rock band. The strength of the team is agility, improvisation, resilience, and perseverance. It is a collection of very strong personalities – and I can vouch that sometimes a small spark can ignite a big fire. But I love it when, almost without saying anything, the team can readjust to a new situation and react accordingly.

I would like to have written much more about my team in this book and given them the full credit that they deserve. Unfortunately I am pressed for space, but rest assured they are the real stars of the show.

The opinions here are my own, and do not represent the official position of SWIFT scrl, my employer at the time of publication of this book, in any way.

Except where noted, photos and artwork © by Konstantin (Kosta) Peric.

PART 1
INTRODUCTION

A small body of determined spirits fired
by an unquenchable faith in their mission
can alter the course of history
(MAHATMA GANDHI)

CHAPTER 1
KEY DEFINITIONS

THE CLASSIC definitions of innovation include:

1. The process of making improvements by introducing something new.
2. A new idea, method or device.
3. Change that creates a new dimension of performance.

While invention is a new product, innovation is a new value. Individuals and organisations often blur the distinction.

Another key definition in this book is open innovation.

"Open innovation is a paradigm that assumes that firms can and should use external ideas as well as internal ideas, and internal and external paths to market, as the firms look to advance".

For the purpose of this book, I use the word innovation to denote the process of bringing an idea to fruition.

Fruition can mean commercial success, cost reduction in a process, adoption. In other words, it is a measure of the tangible or intangible value brought to the observers and users of the result.

Not all ideas are good ideas. Many ideas will not make it to any fruition. Even then, the value of these ideas is that we can learn from their failure. Some ideas will evolve and change many times in the process of fruition.

CHAPTER 2

WHAT IS THIS BOOK ABOUT?

THIS BOOK could have been the story of Innotribe.

The story of how SWIFT, a banking co-operative based near Brussels, developed over 4 years to become an innovation leader. On this journey SWIFT changed the broader global financial community.

But as I started writing this story I realised that there was a much bigger story beyond it.

For those of you less familiar with the financial services world – here is what you need to know about SWIFT.

SWIFT sets the standards for international financial transactions, and runs a highly secure and reliable network (or intranet), connecting 8,000 banks and 1,500 major corporations across the globe. The motto of the company is FNAO – "Failure is not an option". It's quite a natural sentiment if you consider that even a couple of seconds of downtime could have a major impact. The world looks to SWIFT for reliability and delivery.

As the head of innovation at SWIFT, and proud co-creator of the Innotribe, I usually take the role of front man. I have told this story many times – sometimes as an "elevator pitch" in an actual elevator, sometimes with journalists, peer heads of innovation, bankers, movers and shakers, government ministers, venture capitalists. I've blogged for the world to read.

Very often, people tell me about their optimism in seeing "the beating heart of innovation, in the heart of Europe and the financial industry". They might even mention the revival in collaborative spirit, the delivery of new products and services and forming a community around values such as honesty and transparency.

So here goes ...

This book is definitely not a corporate history of SWIFT or even the story of Innotribe.

So what is this book about?

It is:

- A manual for company innovation.
- A personal development guide for those wanting to get involved in innovation, and wondering how to start.
- A guide to bringing the values and passion of a start-up to an established company.
- A guide to the forces shaping our world, and how to work with them.
- A rebuttal to the myths that surround innovation.

In writing this book, I've faced some real problems and trade-offs.

I am aware that:

- Managers and leaders looking to organise innovation from a strategic, corporate governance, human resources, organisational design or operational research perspective are probably less interested in the 'personal journey' aspects.

- That the personal details of great value to me and my team will be less meaningful to those with no direct experience of Innotribe or finance.
- That some of the future-looking initiatives and academic theory will be irrelevant or obscure to people currently dealing with work problems.
- That what is relevant to very young and new employees might not be informative to CEOs.

I have deliberately not written a traditional book. My motivation is to bring some magic, buzz and vitality to this most traditional of formats, in the same way that I've tried to revive conferences as tools for collaboration and innovation (as you will see later on). I try and be punchy and engaging throughout. And, for a book that is about innovation and collaboration I draw frequently on the people that have inspired and influenced me on my journey. I am very lucky as I am constantly networking with some of the best and brightest people around, it's this knowledge that I try hard to convey. As a consequence the book has the odd tangent, but then again, so do most innovation projects!

Although I try hard to make this an easy book to follow, similar to a lecture or a seminar, for you the reader, this will only be a worthwhile exercise if you are asking some very hard questions of yourself.

As I write throughout the book, *how you do* it is as important as what you do. So this book is many things, but it is not boring!

I understand that many of you will come to this book looking for tools and techniques and ideas, and yes, they are provided. But I must warn you that tools and techniques are not sufficient for themselves. Most innovation initiatives end in failure (ideally it should be controlled failure) so ultimately you should have the ability to:

- Manage yourself
- Keep faith in the innovation process
- Have others keep faith in you.

This is what determines your success.

So it's about character and resilience, not your knowledge of ideas and case studies. For this reason I have maintained some 'narrative and detail', as they represent the reality of what you will daily come up against.

But even if the entire book isn't for you, some or most of it will be. In writing this book I have tried my hardest to be inclusive and to keep jargon, in particular financial jargon, to a minimum. But if I have failed to do this, then please feel free to email or tweet me your comments.

CHAPTER 3
WHAT'S THE PROBLEM WITH INNOVATION IN ESTABLISHED COMPANIES?

MY MOTIVATION for writing this book is that the story I tell is *repeatable.*

And it *needs to be*, because while banking is a highly regulated, conservative and slow moving industry, *it's not the only one.* So if all I do with this book is reach the converted in the financial services industry (much as I love them), then I have failed. Reflecting on that last comment, I have to say that given the bad publicity that banking has attracted over the last few years, if the industry was to really focus itself on innovation, and was perceived to have the same commitment to design excellence that a company like Apple does, then perhaps the public would be more forgiving of our mistakes.

I work with heads of innovation in large organisations all over the world.

The same story always emerges.

In many established companies it is difficult to innovate, as the main focus is often on the optimisation of processes and cost reduction. So it is very difficult for people to experiment with new ideas, which often fail.

Heads of Innovation are often better regarded in *other* organisations than in their own. In a way this is very good for me, as many heads of innovation have provided case studies and ideas to use in this book. These I have added and have made all examples suitably anonymous.

Universities, schools, governments, healthcare, publishing, just a few examples of industries needing to go through the same process that I've been through with banking and financial services. But while these are very different industries, the underlying forces are often the same.

Governments? You ask. Here is what space entrepreneur James Bennett recently wrote about government:

> 'Governmental agencies by their nature tend to avoid innovation unless they are operating under the extraordinary pressure of war or the threat of war.
>
> In normal times, the bureaucrat is rewarded primarily for avoiding trouble and penalized for anything that draws negative attention to his higher-ups. An innovation that succeeds and saves money or otherwise benefits the government is typically not rewarded; thus the bureaucrat is rewarded for avoiding innovation.
>
> The government is particularly poor at imagining new uses of a thing and presenting it in a way that it catches on voluntarily.
>
> Private enterprise is good at such things, and investors are constantly seeking innovation.'

James is a US libertarian. He is an amazing guy, whose commercial ventures have been funded by amongst others, a famous rock star, and his knowledge of the government, military and the Cold War could have been the basis for several episodes of the X Files. But even if you find his comments slightly harsh, perhaps you would agree that there is a need to find a mid-point where conservative institutions and enterprise can meet?

Here are some comments from a recent Innotribe meeting in Belfast.

Arlene Foster, Northern Ireland minister of enterprise, trade and investment and Steve Van Wyk, CIO at ING talked about how to instil and foster innovation in large companies, governments and countries. I was honoured they used my "Castle and the Sandbox" metaphor – if the core business of an established company is the "castle" (well protected and built to last), innovation is best carried out in "sandboxes" – environments outside the castle where experimentation with new ideas and concepts is easier. Eventually ideas in the sandbox will become products and services that can be brought back to the castle. Steve used the "ING Direct" example in the United States as a good example of a sandbox experiment.

Arlene Foster then talked about the concept of open innovation and explored how that can be used to crowd-source ideas for the government, increasing positive politics and interactions and reducing bureaucracy and hierarchies. She impressed me – I haven't heard such talk in politics in a long time, or even ever.

I believe this experience can be reproduced in other established companies, even those that are less inclined to be innovative.

CHAPTER 4

BIG DATA: AN EXAMPLE OF
A MISSED OPPORTUNITY

Big Data is one of the forces defining our age, and yet most established organisations are unable to leverage it. I think it's because it's one of these big "transversal" ideas for which it is very difficult to find an owner in our typical silos and hierarchical organisations.

What does Big Data mean? I hand you over to mobile financial services entrepreneur and legend Carol Realini.

Today, what is increasing most rapidly is the amount of online data that exists about us.

We spend more time online, there are more types of personal information offered and gathered, and countless applications are saving all this information.

Google keeps your searches.

Facebook knows your friends.

Your mobile network operator knows whom you call, where you are, and when you travel.

Sony knows how good you are at video games.

As we use more applications and interact with more connected devices, the world of Big Data only gets bigger and bigger.

Harnessed in the right way, this growing mass of highly granular data can improve our consumer and life experience significantly.

Many business models are built around monetizing data, usually through advertising. And the more data they have, along with more interactions comes more potential for monetization.

Advertisers want results, and they get much better results if their ads are targeted with precision. Now with real-time geographical location as part of Big Data, they can even reach out with an ad or an offer based on where we are at any given moment.

Another use for Big Data is to make more sophisticated credit decisions. FICA scores are based on a limited number of historical data sources. A new credit scoring system could leverage a lot more information and help lenders make smarter, more relevant decisions. It can also be used for micro decisions – using real time data to make short-term decisions.

So if we follow Carol's reasoning it would appear that Big Data is a really good thing. But are companies able to exploit it?

Carol answers this question with reference to financial services in America

Why have US superbanks been slow to adopt Big Data strategies?

A cynic might suggest that they don't feel any urgency.

But a knowledgeable pragmatist would understand that a major contributing factor is the fragmentation of the business. Superbanks have a lot of data, but it tends to reside in compartmentalised departments or silos, and is difficult to access across firewalls. They have contracts with networks like Visa that limit their use of information, and regulations and consumer agreements may limit their use. These are major obstacles, but they can be overcome. And if overcome, they can be used to improve the efficiency of the business, personalize how the banks interact with their customers, provide new business models, and enable smarter credit decisions.

Could be a gold mine.

In the meantime, the world around banking is taking advantage of Big Data and starting the process of disintermediating the existing players. This next example, provided by Canadian entrepreneur and marketing guru Mark Sibthorpe picks up from where Carol left the story. For those of you who are less familiar with credit and loyalty and find this a bit 'jargon heavy' get in touch and I'll help out as best as I can!

What do MasterCard and Billy Beane have in common?

Analytics
In the book by Michael Lewis, 'Moneyball, The Art of Winning an Unfair Game', the author focused on the flaws that existed in the traditional way baseball management evaluated player performance. Major League Baseball (MLB) managers before Billy Beane used gut feel, intuition and experience in place of facts that could be backed up by data (player stats). Even today with all of the tools available to marketers, there are still many examples where gut feel makes the call.

MasterCard, on the other hand, with its recent purchase of Truaxis, sees an alternative. Truaxis, and a slew of other competitors, lets merchants attract new prospect by precisely targeting consumers that match the criteria set by a merchant, the idea being to create relevant offers without deep discounts normally associated with daily deals. It targets the offers by combining a number of variables such as purchase history and location, the data captured each time a cardholder makes a purchase.

This approach is a significant leap over other offered solutions because merchants are able to target specific types of consumers, and success can be measured because the transaction data is captured at the point of sale (POS).

For example, take a merchant wishing to attract clients from a competing convenience store. Card-linked-rewards make this possible. A merchant could select prospects that frequent 7-11, have done a transaction within 60 days and are located within three miles of designated locations.

Once selected, prospects get pushed an offer. If the offer is redeemed, the data is captured at the POS or by the issuer. Exact details of a transaction are tracked, including subsequent visits. This eliminates any guesswork, giving marketers the necessary tools required to measure the return on investment. In fact, marketers can't lose as they only pay for proven results.

Why is this such a big deal?

It's a huge deal because merchants can target consumers based on transaction data without having to invest in proprietary loyalty systems to do it. In addition, merchants can target participants outside their own client base.

In the past, this meant dishing out significant amounts of money either to build a co-brand program or set up a loyalty program. Tesco's is a great example of what this can mean to a merchant's bottom line. It is well documented how Tesco pioneered traditional single-merchant loyalty programs and its 'Clubcard' program was the grocer's equivalent to Moneyball 7 years before Beane changed the way MLB was managed.

If that's too complicated just think "Moneyball!"

A lot of people associate innovation with new products, like a phone or a tablet computer, but actually it's as much about new processes and approaches as it is about products.

So if we agree with what Carol and Mark write, what are the steps to take us to a new form of organisation that facilitates new, emerging opportunities? I look at this in the next chapter.

CHAPTER 5
THE INGREDIENTS FOR INNOVATION

In my view the ingredients of success are:

- Embracing open innovation – ideas to improve or revolutionise your business can come from everywhere, from other industries, from Hollywood, and not only from your marketing people or labs.
- Establishing an environment where it is safe to experiment and fail, and establishing a process governing this environment, in particular how the products get, or do not get, back into your core business.
- Providing a comprehensive, bottom-up, communication platform to keep everyone aware of innovation processes and initiatives.
- Engaging and supporting your employees on the innovation path.
- Establishing a highly motivated and diverse innovation team to lead the transformation, and getting executive support for it.

Combining these ingredients in a way that suits your company is necessary to initiate the innovation transformation.

You will also need patience, perseverance and passion.

CHAPTER 6
WHY DO WE HAVE TO INNOVATE?

I LOVE METAPHORS, and I will use a Hollywood one to illustrate why innovation is needed in established industries and companies.

Recently I watched the film "The Artist".

It's a movie by Michel Hazanivicius with Jean Dujardin and Bérénice Bejo. I recommend it highly for its idea, visual style, and the beautiful acting performances. The movie won many Oscars, and is the first ever non-Anglo-Saxon movie to win the best movie award.

The story is of a silent movie star facing the advent of the sound movies, all in the context of the 1929 crisis.

The character – George Valentin – does not understand the new technology, has not seen it coming, and in fact doesn't understand why the change is happening. His idea of the beauty and artistic value of silent movies is losing ground.

It struck me that's where the banking industry is today.

There is an established order, arguably centuries old, about how banks process money and loans and the products and services they provide.

But the banks are under pressure:

- The on-going crisis
- The new connected generation using social media
- The advent of easy, cheap person-to-person international payments (Paypal and others)
- New business models, dubbed banking 2.0 (e.g. Movenbank, Simple, Fidorbank)
- The arrival of telecom operators as payment processors (mobile payment schemes not involving banks)

But in the movie, George doesn't see it. Perhaps he doesn't WANT to see it. And so the new movies "happen to him", *in the same way as "digital banking" may happen to established players.*

I don't want to spoil the movie for you, so a very quick summary. Eventually George, with the help of Peppy Miller (played wonderfully well by Bérénice Bejo), realises the predicament he is in. He can't cope with the full change of things, but he adapts and in the end rides the wave of change, in his own unique way.

This ending perfectly fits my eternally optimistic take.

I do think that if banks (and others) realise the massive change taking place, they can ride the wave and better serve the connected generation, to enable them to manage their digital assets (and not only money).

For the doubters, I can only point to the recent demise of Kodak, as well as Nokia and Microsoft's recent troubles in competing with the iPhone. Let's look at 'The Kodak problem', as set out by John Naughton in The Observer from January 2012:

> Kodak is like Coca-Cola, a brand-name that defined an industry.
>
> One of its products – the colour film Kodachrome – even became the title of one of Paul Simon's most famous songs.
>
> You can't get more iconic than that.
>
> And the company was an industrial giant – at one time (1976), for example, it had 90% of film and 85% of camera sales in the US and was regularly rated one of the world's five most valuable brands.
>
> So it seemed inconceivable that a company as large and successful could disappear. And yet...

The article goes on to say that one of the ideas that proved disruptive to Kodak had originally emerged out of its own research.

So it can happen to the biggest and (once) the best.

You know, I'm sure that there were people who worked at Kodak and saw what they did as a job and nothing more, but I'm sure that there were many more that loved the company and would have done anything to make it thrive. I'm sure that there were also many dedicated, very busy employees who couldn't see beyond the day-to-day. Who can blame them? Working out 'innovation future' is very hard. I turn again to James Bennett:

> The Danish physicist Niels Bohr famously observed "prediction is very difficult, especially about the future". Gifted and less ambitious futurists prefer to confine themselves to generating scenarios. It's possible to identify possibilities, and pathways, and critical decision points. There are, of course, a thousand reasons why the actual outcome may be something entirely unanticipated, but we cannot help that.

> A futurist in the year 1946 asked to predict the next forty years of radio and electronics would have diligently examined all the constraining factors on progress in electronics and come up with a variety of scenarios, and they probably would have been a reasonable range by the understanding of that day. And they would have been entirely useless, and certainly wrong – all of them -- because he would not have, and could not have predicted the discovery of the transistor, which seemed to violate the known laws of physics at that time. Much of his work would have been based on estimating the ultimate limits of development of the vacuum tube, which in turn would have determined the ultimate limits of size and speed of any electronic device envisioned.

> It is possible that estimating the next ten years of industry development will be just as futile. By definition, we cannot

predict with confidence. All we can do is lay out scenarios and try to assign probabilities to them, hoping they are realistic.

Now here's another question. How many Kodak employees were users of the very products that caused Kodak's decline? I turn again to Carol Realini, to reframe this question in terms of the US auto and banking industries:

> In many ways, New York today is like Detroit in the 1970s and 1980s. So for a decade after California embraced small imported cars, people in the Midwest continued to buy big American cars.
>
> When everyone working at Ford drives a Ford, it is not surprising that myopia sets in. While Toyota's cars were gaining acceptance with American consumers, it is likely that most autoworkers and executives in Detroit had never seen one up close, much less driven one.
>
> New York is one of the great cities of the world, with unmatched culture and vibrancy. But due to the concentration of money and power within one industry, New York is a company town. It's a banking bubble.

Here's a question that needs a very honest answer: Are you in the bubble?

CHAPTER 7
SOME WORDS FOR THE SCEPTICAL
AND CYNICAL

So what conclusions do you draw from everything so far, and how do you respond? Innovation faces a lot of opposition: from vested interests, people who support the status quo and many others. The sorts of responses I often get include:

"I am not interested, and I certainly don't want to be lectured by a guy from finance, one of the least innovative industries around".

"I do a SWOT analysis once a year, now leave me alone."

"Erm, we already have a product development team."

Do you shrug your shoulders and say, "This is a problem for the CEO, not for me".

"Yes, that's all well and good, but innovation is for people in Silicon Valley or young guys in Harvard dorms. Somehow I'll just muddle through."

Sigh: "I'd love to be involved in this stuff, but my organisation will never allow it".

The last complaint is particularly interesting, and I do sympathise. I do however have a bigger and better suggestion to people who say this: Why not start a fire outside your organisation? I'll explore this later in the book, but my theory is that the walls separating your company from the outside world are arbitrary.

I'm used to dealing with scepticism, so I hear and see this stuff all the time. Some of the sceptics will remain sceptics forever. But I have seen the method I explain in this book convert a good deal of other sceptics into walking and then running with me. So, read on!

CHAPTER 8
BEING BIG ISN'T GOOD IF IT'S FOR
THE WRONG REASONS

MOST C-LEVEL EXECUTIVES will look at what I have written and come to the conclusion, "Let's get bigger! We'll acquire, we'll create economies of scale, we'll be safe, and we'll be too big to fail."

Well, OK.

But the evidence doesn't support this anymore. Mike Guillaume is an expert on this subject. He's a guy who studies company reports for a living and is based not far from SWIFT, so I turn to him for support in assessing why mergers and acquisitions are not the answer to your problem.

In the first half of the 1990s there were more than 1,500 mergers in the U.S. financial sector alone. There can be good motives behind mergers, acquisitions, or other more flexible forms of joint ventures: increased revenues; larger market share; economies of scale or of scope; critical size; access to new markets, diversification; synergies; vertical integration, etc. However, too many M&As seem to be driven by a fear of being left behind, or by a bad desire, or a clear design, to choke off rivals; or even by a runaway solution to internal problems.

According to the maverick management guru Tom Peters: "Bigger is almost never better. Big mergers are stupid. [They] spring naturally from big egos. At times of market uncertainty, the biggies, even the so-called "good" biggies, bulk up to defend themselves... And yet we do "it" again and again..."[1] Summarising the reasons why M&As are, on the whole, less than successful, would take an entire book. It boils down to at least six explanations, at work alone or together:

- An ill-conceived business model;
- A wrong fit (between products, cultures, et al.);
- Embedded problems in the acquired company;
- An ill-advised financial structure (mind the investment bankers here, too!);
- A decrease in market responsiveness (internal or "digestion" concerns being put first and slowing down reactive capabilities);
- A wrong timing – or sudden or unplanned change – in the business, industry or economic environment that make the "best" plan go down – or makes things worse.

This sequence is almost invariably repeated:

A company is not great simply because it is big. Small can be beautiful, and often delivers better results.[2] Spinoffs, buyouts (by management and employees) and IPOs from larger companies are more flexible and often fare much better than they did as internal divisions, whatever the industry.

---

1   Tom Peters: "26 Rules for Recessions", posted on June 30, 2008 on www.tompeters. com.

2   See the article written by Catherine Armst on www.businessweek.com: "Drug Mergers: Killers for Research" (March 9, 2009). What has the complete acquisition of the smaller Genentech by its larger parent Roche brought to both parties? And so on...

Is being big always bad? Certainly not, as in a number of industries, size can be a critical factor for success. In addition, growing externally is not inherently a recipe for doom. Still, caution is recommended as is concern over side-effects.

An example from big pharma

Early in 2009, Pfizer's CEO told the Financial Times that his company was considering the acquisition of a "large rival" to improve its financial health, adding that "The real goal is to grow revenues" and that, naturally, it should (sic) "meet the criteria of shareholder value."[3] That says much about one of today's worrying trends in the system: being bigger for the sake of it, and doing this by acquiring competitors instead of trying to grow your own revenues – and innovate – by your own means.

Having been conservative for decades with regard to external growth, and epitomizing large-scale innovative entrepreneurship with William Steere at the helm, Pfizer then embarked on a frantic buying spree.[4] Numbers mattered. In 1990, sales were $4,757 million, ROE (return on equity) was 16.9 percent, EPS (Earnings Per Share) were $0.17. In 1999, sales were up to $14,135 million, ROE had more than doubled to 35.9 percent, and EPS reached $0.85. For those who pay more attention to market value, this had jumped from $3.37 per share to $32.44 over the same period.

Then came the 2000s.

The share price halved between 1999 and 2007, resulting in a $140 billion fall in corporate value. Sure, as an immediate effect

---

3   January 5, 2009.

4   See performance indicators as reported in Pfizer annual reports from 1991 to 2000, from which our figures were sourced. Incidentally, or coincidentally, it is worth noting that the quality of information (and the number of ratios) in annual reports started decreasing in the early 2000s.

of acquisitions, revenues almost tripled in six years. End-2007 EPS were at $1.19, i.e., progressing less than over a comparable period based on organic growth. What about the ever-important ROE? After a mysterious surge to 55.2 percent in 2002, it fell back to a 15 percent average for the last five years. Less than one month after Pfizer's announced intention, this led to the planned purchase of rival Wyeth for $68 billion, with $22.5 billion coming from a consortium of banks... and a dividend cut (with that "shareholder value" still in mind, we assume!). Has the drug giant learned from its past errors? Three years after that huge purchase, Pfizer was considering plans to spin off its animal health division, in which it is still a world market leader. The goal was "to streamline activities after investor criticism over poor returns."[5] A euphemism for saying that the company has become too big to be manageable.

To be fair, Pfizer is far from being the sole company in its industry to have demonstrated an addiction to size: consider e.g. GlaxoSmithKline (GSK), whose full name should now be (take a deep breath), Burroughs-Wellcome-Glaxo-Laboratories-Smithkline-Beecham, had imaginative (?) brand experts not shortened the company identity after its numerous acquisitions and mergers.

Small, beautiful, and more than that

> "Any intelligent fool can make things bigger, more complex, and more violent. It takes a touch of genius – and a lot of courage – to move in the opposite direction," wrote E.F. Schumacher.[6]

A small enterprise can indeed be a beautiful thing. Lest some forget it, real entrepreneurs pay themselves with (a part of)

---

5 "Pfizer talks to banks about unit's $3bn part-flotation" (Financial Times, February 20, 2012).

6 Ernst Friedrich Schumacher: "*Small is beautiful. a study of economics as if people mattered*" *(Blond & Briggs, 1973).*

the bottom line, which says it all. That makes a difference, not only in size and style, but also in behaviour. As the American psychologist David McClelland says, an entrepreneur's key motivation is the need for achievement and an urge to build. Entrepreneurship has its thrills and spills. And the virtues – and competitive advantages – of a small enterprise are real:

- Structure is flatter and less complex;
- Communication is more simple;
- Decision-making process is quicker;
- Customer drive is much stronger;
- Flexibility is higher.

A number of medium-sized companies also display much greater innovation capabilities than big ones.[7] So much so that an unwritten law of capitalism is that most product and technological breakthroughs comes from outside large corporations and dominating groups. The then relatively small Apple and Microsoft drove a few computer giants out of the market and forced a company like IBM to adapt.[8]

SMEs are the biggest job generators, with 65-75 percent of existing jobs and 80-90 percent of new jobs created by small companies in most economies (in India, half of GDP comes from SMEs). Big also happens to see smaller as better: the global value of corporate spin-offs has doubled from 2011 to 2012 to reach $400 billion, highlighting an increasing trend for

---

7 "Innovation and Entrepreneurship. Practice and Principles" is the title of a management book written in 1985 by Peter F. Drucker that still makes compelling reading (HarperCollins, 1985). Read also: "Innovation: The Attacker's Advantage" by Richard N. Foster (Summit Books, 1986).

8 After years of domination of the computer and software industry (with market shares over 60 percent in some segments, i.e., well behind what Microsoft's current share), IBM saw its core business shrink, its then CEO declaring he was "mad at losing market shares," and reported in fiscal year 1992 what was then the biggest loss in U.S. corporate history. It took years to turn the giant around, but it had to shed a large part of its core activities.

large companies to refocus their business by disposing of non-core assets.

A small enterprise can also turn into a dreadful experience.

However, small-scale production, distribution and services are the keys to a renewed economic model.

CHAPTER 9
HOW BIG AND SMALL CAN WORK TOGETHER

THE "SIZE DOES MATTER" economic model that prevails today often means internal inertial forces become stronger than healthy external market pressure. Becoming too big, too slow, too fat, less flexible, less responsive, and less agile are risks faced by many firms, and a cause of failure for some.

So growing and merging your way out of a crisis isn't always an option.

Sometimes companies need to be big and old and sometimes they are smaller and new.

But my interest is in the positive and the optimistic. These are the points at which big and small can meet, and are opportunities for open collaboration and learning.

My suggestion, as you may have guessed, is for a journey of cultural change.

If you're scared of the start-up companies in your industry, this implies that you think that they might disrupt you. OK, not everyone likes changes, but what is the really rational, sensible, business response? Surely you would want to know more about what they're doing, perhaps even: Working with them? Funding them? Advising them?

How do you think they see you?

- With contempt?
- With fear?
- With envy?

I think they want your help.

In the last section of the book I take a look at life in a couple of start-ups and I think it might surprise you. Here are the comments from Pam Cytron, CEO of Pendo Systems, one of the start-ups I work with:

> The Innotribe program in our eyes is a must.
>
> We don't want to be "too small to succeed deemed by those too big to fail" – this program truly gives a fighting chance not only to Pendo but also to the other firms trying to make a difference to the financial services world.

The fear of the small vendor must be changed or innovation will die.

Are you aware that many large organisations have processes in place that stop small vendors being able to work with them?

CHAPTER 10
VALUES; PASSION AND OR PRAGMATISM

I'M A BIG FAN of science-fiction literature in general, and a genre called cyberpunk in particular, started by a writer called William Gibson and his *Neuromancer* book.

The world depicted by Gibson is one of pervasive hyper-connectivity (based on a successor to the Internet he calls the Grid, that people can hook into using all their senses, creating a sensorial virtual reality), attacked on the edge by hackers diverting the technology for all sorts of uses not foreseen originally. (I even tried to get William Gibson to an Innotribe event, it didn't work. He couldn't understand why I was inviting him to a financial industry event. But hey, it's all about trying.) The spirit of his work inspires me and informs some of the values of my work and the values of innovation. These values are:

- Collaboration
- Intrapreneurship
- Entrepreneurship
- Agility
- Experimentation
- Opening minds to the outside world
- The sense of belonging to a tribe.

And it can be fun.

In this current work environment, people might not associate work with fun, and they might not want to be seen having fun at work, but work can and should be fun.

It's all about passion, and fun is one of the things that ignites passion. Perhaps fun in the workplace has become synonymous with the antics of 'The Office' bosses, Michael Scott in America, David Brent in Britain, but it doesn't have to be this way. Heads of Innovation who set staff up on 'Jack Bauer' missions or on covert ops often get great results. But if you think this approach is frivolous, let me tell you that the *style of your operation* is of great importance, and is the best way to promote a new venture such as an innovation hub. I often capture information using pictures and drawings, because I think that not all moods and ideas can be captured by words alone and there are many people who learn via the visual – you'll be seeing my pictures throughout the book. As was observed at an Innotribe event, 'language barriers persist until we all speak Globish'.

But if passion *really isn't your thing*, perhaps you can try pragmatism.

A blogger I follow closely is Simon Deane-Johns, a London lawyer who co-founded the successful P2P company ZOPA. As Simon writes in his book *"Lipstick on a Pig"*.

> A pragmatist is simply someone who acts in an informed way to control his or her personal environment, using a combination of theory and practice.

> A pragmatist does not slavishly follow rules, or political dogma, or "positive thinking" or the herd. To do so would assume a world that is somehow ordered, whereas almost all significant events in history are Black Swans – surprise events that have a huge impact and which we rationalise by hindsight. Rules and dogma can turn out to be badly wrong.

The herd is eventually caught out. So it's dangerous to follow. Instead, we must rely on experience and critical thought to minimise our exposure to the downside of these surprise events, and maximise our exposure to the upside.

The combination of theory and practice that qualifies as "intelligent practice" involves trial and failure. And this giant, boundaryless online community of practising individuals and facilitators characterises the "architecture of participation" that lies at the heart of "Web 2.0".

It's perhaps no surprise that the rise of Web 2.0 has coincided with a decline and low levels of trust in our institutions, and findings that the level of alienation felt towards politicians, the main political parties and the key institutions of the political system is extremely high and widespread [yet...] very large numbers of citizens are engaged in community and charity work outside of politics. There is also clear evidence that involvement in pressure politics – such as signing petitions, supporting consumer boycotts, joining campaign groups – has been growing significantly for many years.

In other words, it may be that institutions are being marginalised by people pragmatically engaging with each other in their own digital communities, not only for retail purposes but also political, environmental, health, and economic reasons.

Big questions arise:

- How do the institutions get it so wrong?
- How do facilitators succeed where institutions fail?
- How can we bridge the gap between what institutions say is right for us, and what is actually right for us personally?
- Could today's successful facilitators become tomorrow's institutions?
- Are today's institutions doomed?

So which side are you on? And as the optimist, I think there is a place for Simon's pragmatism to work with my approach. In the last section of the book I explore the topic of banks for a better world.

But if you're really too cool to be passionate, then try channelling your pragmatism! And if you are a true pragmatist, you'll have read the chapter on mergers and the one on Big Data, and will have concluded that innovation is as rational a response as any.

In some ways I am lucky in that the finance community has more access to funding than many conservative industries, (the charity sector being one example), and people will say:

"You have achieved all this, but that's because you have all this time, support and budget. In my company I'm lucky if the boss gives me budget for the train ticket to the next town."

To this I reply: funding is always welcome, and support from the top of the organisation is even more so, but the core value in this story is the *passion of my team*, and the way that they were able to use it and connect with others. Having a large budget does not guarantee that you will create an identity or capture the imagination of the people around you.

My belief is that the passion of the intrapreneur or the entrepreneur is as important, if not more, than the idea itself or the budget available. A passionate person will see the idea through the many inevitable obstacles, drawbacks and disappointments.

But yes, I am fortunate to have the opportunities that I do. Much of this book is given over to discussing the great people whom I have come across as part of Innotribe, I reference them, and give contact details, so why not get in touch with them? I'm sure they would like to help intrapraneurs and entrepreneurs everywhere. Certainly I'm sure you'll have better feedback than I got from William Gibson!

CHAPTER 11
THE UK'S NATIONAL HEALTH SERVICE, ABSOLUTELY NOTHING TO DO WITH FINANCIAL SERVICES

VERY DELIBERATELY, I turn away from the financial community to make my concluding comments in this introduction.

Although I'm trying to reach the wider business community, I realise that my natural inclination is always to turn to examples from financial services as it's the area I know best. So I've deliberately put in a case study that has nothing at all to do with banking.

Healthcare is alongside banking – perhaps more important than banking – one of the industries that underpins modern, civilised society.

Healthcare is provided in different ways in different societies. Measuring healthcare outcomes and success is notoriously difficult as there are so many variables. I focus here on the NHS (National Health System) that operates in the UK.

The NHS has been described as the nearest thing that the UK has to a 'national religion', and if you remember, it was the breakout star from the opening ceremony of the London Olympics!

So my thanks to Danny Boyle for getting me started on this subject.

While I want to keep away from the political aspects of this discussion, I think that it highlights many of the structural and organisational issues that I make in this book about adapting, connecting and innovating in established organisations and traditional industries.

So here goes ...

The challenges facing the NHS now are very different from when it was first established (1948), and how the NHS is organised has changed, partly influenced by the changes in other large-scale organisations. There is now a more commercial approach then hitherto, and more delegation to individual units.

The current debate about privatisation and the future of the NHS sometimes appears to be assuming the NHS is still organised the way it was by its founders.

This is not the case.

It has developed from an organisation with the specific role of treating illness into the contemporary concept of something that ensures we are healthy, or "health management". The contemporary NHS has evolved into a commissioning service with multi-agency working, and third sector involvement now commonplace.

This could be seen as more involvement of the public and patients as consumers, but it is not the same as these stakeholders influencing how it works.

When the NHS was established in 1948 it incorporated a variety of institutions, all with their own forms of governance and connection with the public. Some hospitals were run by local authorities, others by charities or bodies such as trade unions.

The prevailing philosophy at the time was that a strong central approach was the way to get things done.

The priority at the time was dealing with epidemics and putting right the ravages of the war.

As reform came over many years, it became less clear to the public who was responsible for what.

The way the NHS has been managed has also changed. The old idea in 1948 was very much a centrally controlled organisation, as were other newly nationalised organisations at the time. Tension immediately arose, with demands for local involvement by local authorities and the public and patients.

What does sociological theory can tell us about how organisations like the NHS are run?

Sociological management theory was originally defined within the work of Max Weber.

Weber defined organisation structure through the notion of hierarchy, where promotion was on merit, and each position had clearly defined duties as a "bureaucracy".

Although the word "bureaucratic" now has bad overtones, the development of efficient bureaucracies led to considerable advances in human welfare and happiness.

Writing in early 20th-century Germany, Weber based his ideas on the efficient organisations created by Bismarck which followed military lines. Such a system could produce a large number of products efficiently.

Yet contemporary organisations have evolved into far more complex structures due to globalisation and should be conceptualised through the notion of "post-Fordism". This is due to their complex nature, where a rigid bureaucracy along Weberian lines is no longer viable, and has to be replaced with a decentralised system with an emphasis on outcomes rather than rules.

Although the old Weberian hierarchy may be less evident, post-Fordist power relationships still remain as a mechanism of keeping costs under control. Peter Drucker, the 20th century management theorist developed ideas about the public sector. He suggested that large businesses worked best when they were decentralised, rather than the command and control model (the Weberian idea of a bureaucracy). Businesses and governments have a tendency to cling to "yesterday's successes" rather than seeing they are no longer useful.

Later in his life he became more aware of the importance of the "third sector", the non-profit- making organisation, neither privately nor government-run – what we now call a "social enterprise". He argued that in a more complex society, organisations should be given objectives, and allowed to achieve them in their own way.

In the old fashioned Weberian hierarchy power came down a pyramid. People often "mediated" or adapted instructions to suit their particular circumstances. Now it goes directly from the top to the front line.

The NHS was traditionally seen as a hierarchical organisation in the Weberian and Fordist mould.

Recent work on the NHS has looked at the change from a professionally run NHS, where major decisions were left to the professionals, to a more market–orientated managerial system, where issues of financial accountability and measurement of effectiveness become more salient.

What is happening in the NHS can best be described as a "task culture". Put simply this means that an organisation has to be flexible, and restructure itself to meet new challenges.

Now this is a long case study and does not draw upon my own direct experience (thank you David Taylor-Gooby), but it illustrates all my points about organisational evolution, control and open innovation.

The NHS is a huge, complex and sprawling organisation. It is a castle. How to bring open innovation to the NHS?

My suggestion is to read the rest of the book and then to return to this chapter, and think how you might bring a 'castle and sandbox' approach to such a large, complex, ever evolving organisation.

PART 2
MY BACKGROUND

"As for the future, your task is not to foresee it,
but to enable it."
(Antoine de Saint-Exupéry)

In the previous section I looked at some of the wider issues that sit around innovation. This part sets the background for readers with less experience of my industry, and indeed me.

I explain a little bit more about SWIFT and tell a little about my own time at SWIFT and the creation of Innotribe.

What I want to do is offer some insights into the expectations, practices, cultural background and norms of the industry that I work in.

Even if you don't work in financial services, you will perhaps find some resonance with the issues that you face in your own industry.

Those of you who already know this story, feel free to skip it!

CHAPTER 12
THE PITCH

THE HALLMARK of innovation is the "pitch".

Innovators and entrepreneurs know this – it is one thing to have an idea; it is another thing to make someone buy into it. So innovators and entrepreneurs need to be able to pitch their idea to:

- executives;
- management;
- venture capitalists;
- clients;
- partners, etc.

The pitch needs to be short, sharp, clear, attention catching. In fact, I have noticed over the years that the best pitch is the one showing passion.

Here is, for example, the "Innotribe pitch" in the form of a Q&A. It will help you also understand how the key ideas in this book have been applied in the particular case of Innotribe.

What is Innotribe? How has it been built?

Innotribe is SWIFT's initiative to enable collaborative innovation.

Innotribe enables innovation at SWIFT and in the financial industry of which SWIFT is an integral part.

At SWIFT, we started in 2009 by organising Innovation Challenges – events where anybody working for SWIFT can put forward ideas. The prize is for the winning team to implement their idea. Since then, the innovation challenges and other tools have become part of the tradition at SWIFT. Typically about 10% to 20% of the staff contribute.

In the financial community, we started at Sibos Hong Kong in 2009 by organising the first Innotribe@Sibos- a highly interactive event where the delegates of Sibos could get inspired by industry experts and engage in *ideation* activities. The event culminated in an innovation award for the best idea, which was subsequently funded with a $50,000 prize. Since then, Innotribe@Sibos has become a permanent feature of Sibos. We have also diversified our events outside of Sibos – for example the highly successful Innotribe@Mumbai event in 2011 focused on "connecting the unbanked".

In 2011, the Innotribe program was enhanced with an incubator – a resource for the financial industry and SWIFT to experiment with the implementation of the ideas generated at our events. In 2011, the incubator has produced several new concepts – such as MyStandards.

Also introduced in 2011, the start-up challenge events provide a platform where banks and financial institutions meet the start-up community. The start-up companies highly value this opportunity to get in touch with the financial world, while the financial institutions hugely appreciate a quality selection of start-up companies in which they may potentially invest.

Innotribe values are:

- neutrality;
- authenticity;
- simplicity;
- and passion.

The team at SWIFT behind Innotribe is composed of 10 people, covering a wide range of skills – event design, facilitation and curation, business and technology expertise, program management, marketing.

Above all, Innotribe is a network.

How can innovation help the community face the challenges of the industry?

Innotribe is a forum to discuss issues and trends that are important for the community from the technology, economy and social aspects.

We put "Igniters" (recognised experts and thought leaders) in touch with the financial community, to understand, discuss and design the short, medium and long term responses to emerging trends, including:

- digital identity;
- cloud computing;
- social data and media;
- business intelligence and analytics;
- mobile payments;
- alternative and virtual currencies;
- new economies;
- new organisational modes;
- the hyper-connected generation of people;
- social entrepreneurship support.

Innotribe helps people to understand what is happening and formulate a response.

What are the priorities of your Innovation team?

We are looking to manage a portfolio of innovative projects:

- Incremental innovation: develop new products and services that SWIFT can provide to the community – the EBAM Hub product (single window multi-bank electronic bank account management service for corporate clients).

- New business model innovation: incubate the idea for a SWIFT provided "financial app store" supporting the financial community – where banks, third parties and SWIFT can provide application services to the 10,000+ strong community connected to SWIFTNet.

- Disruptive innovation: the "digital asset grid", a concept where banks would evolve their services to provide digital asset management products in addition to money and fund management, and "Banks for a better world", a collaborative initiative to bridge the traditional finance and social finance worlds.

What is the objective of "The Innovation Sandbox" and how does it work?

An "innovation sandbox", such as Innotribe's incubator, is a place where a company sets aside resources (time, money, location, legal and brand protection) to enable their internal entrepreneurs to explore their ideas in a "safe" environment. Safe means that the sandbox is isolated so that failure does not affect the main company brand, reputation, or core products and business. In the case of the SWIFT Incubator, we manage six to eight projects each year.

What are the keys to success when innovating in companies? How can we encourage innovative initiatives/ projects within a company?

The key success factors are:

- Embracing ideas, not only from inside your company but also from outside – clients, partners, people at large. This is the "open" innovation concept, one of the cornerstones of Innotribe.
- Enabling the intra/entrepreneurs experiment in a safe environment. This is the "innovation sandbox" concept.

CHAPTER 13
HOW I GOT THERE

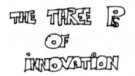

"Energy and persistence conquer all things"
(BENJAMIN FRANKLIN)

Some background on SWIFT and me.

I joined SWIFT in 1990 in the "Corporate Research" department. This was quite a sizable unit of about 35 people, split into two areas of research – artificial intelligence and telecommunications. I joined the telecommunication side of the unit, as a database architect and designer. My focus was on message standards.

At SWIFT, standards are a hallmark and key value (along with security and resilience – more on these later). Indeed standards are the glue of the financial community, making transactions go straight through with certainty and no manual interventions. Consider that on the SWIFT network, Citi will immediately process a payment instruction from a regional bank in Fiji without asking questions.

Back at that time, standards were designed by a diverse bunch of people – historians, biologists, and journalists. So I developed a methodology for message design based on software engineering techniques from the database world.

In the two years I spent in research, my work had lots of success outside of SWIFT, but very little inside.

I was learning one of the basic rules of innovation – for each idea its own time. It would indeed turn out that my work from that time would be picked up much later and become the basis of how standards are designed today. I was also sensing that it was time to move on from research if I wanted to make a career at SWIFT, so I went on to software development and eventually to architect SWIFTNet, the network still running today.

When Lazaro Campos took the reins of SWIFT as CEO in February 2007 he asked me what would be my dream job in a new SWIFT. I said to Lazaro that my thing was innovation;

advanced products and technologies with a small but very capable and talented team. He replied he wanted to establish an innovation group, whose primary goal would be to focus on finding solutions to his three key challenges:

- Reducing the Total Cost of Ownership (TCO) of SWIFT;
- Making SWIFT easier to use, and;
- Making SWIFT more innovative.

Let's see these three challenges in more detail. Understanding them requires understanding the way SWIFT operates and is governed. Understanding them will also highlight approaches to changing company culture.

SWIFT's motto was then, and still is now , "FNAO" – failure is not an option. So, the products were of "military-grade" security (as described by users) as opposed to many other systems out there. In addition, our systems are required to be deployed in configurations that can sustain two major failures and still be able to function.

But in 2007, dissenting voices started coming from these more mainstream operators in the back offices: do we really need all of this complexity? Is it in proportion to the risk and volumes?

The other big issue was the so-called "standards release".

SWIFT is, first and foremost, a standards body.

All the inter-bank and corporate-to-bank transactions obey these standards, with the benefit of "straight-through-processing" or full automation. The advantages of this standardisation are somewhat offset by the fact that, of course, standards need to change in time to comply with new regulations and needs. Thus, every year, SWIFT and the community manage and perform an elaborate program called standards release, culminating every November, on a particular day, in the activation of the new standards. This program in fact results in thousands of projects, within all the vendors and member banks, to implement the required changes in the SWIFT and internal systems. And all vendors and member banks must comply with this mandatory change.

Many wild estimates have been formulated as to how much the standards release process costs the industry. The common point between these estimates is the scale – billions of dollars. And, in 2007, some voices in the community started asking whether these costs couldn't somehow be reduced.

Of course, the 2008 crisis that was yet to come would amplify these rumblings.

So Lazaro wanted to make a big change, and we came up with a surgical strike approach. We devised three projects to tackle the issues from three different directions.

The first was easier access for smaller clients. In 2007, there was an increased need to connect smaller players in the financial industry, to increase the effect of "straight-through processing". So we came up with "Lite". As the name implies, this would be a solution for smaller users that would be Web-based, easier to operate and overall considerably cheaper.

The two other directions were on "cost of ownership". One idea to reduce complexity and cost was to insource customer systems within SWIFT. While promising, this idea was eventually dropped. The other was to reduce the impact of standards releases by providing a tool to shield internal systems from the changes – this would later become the "Integrator" product.

So, in 2007, we set out to develop these projects, and the decision was taken that the innovation team would carry them out. As such, the innovation team was naturally placed into the Products division, and I hand-picked the team that would do this – a small, squad-sized team, of 8 people I trusted and knew they could help me deliver on these challenges.

The idea of the innovation team at that time was to be "black ops" – that is to say, a number of constraints and limits with which other development teams had to comply were lifted as regards these projects. The rationale for this was rooted in one observation and one perception.

The observation was that the products to be developed were different in nature from the "classical" products. For example, in the case of Lite, we didn't have the usual 99.999% availability requirement, as very small players simply didn't need it. For the insourcing project, this model was totally new to SWIFT because we never had a product of such a nature.

The perception was that if we followed the established rules and practices, development would take the traditional one to two years to get to the market, which was much longer than Lazaro wanted. So indeed the projects were carried out in "black ops", special operations mode. In the end, except for the insourcing project that was frozen, two new products hit the market in a record time (under a year from inception to delivery to the customers in pilot) and, by implication, SWIFT could respond to some of the growing concerns.

For the team, though, these were hard times. It was clear that we couldn't continue in the "black ops" mode. And it was clear that this mode wouldn't result in SWIFT becoming more innovative, which was the third of Lazaro's objectives when he took over as CEO.

As the Lite and Integrator projects were nearing delivery, I was looking for new ideas for the innovation team.

A key insight was provided to me by Guido Petit from Alcatel-Lucent in Belgium. He was explaining how his company organised "entrepreneurial boot camps". The management team of Alcatel-Lucent operated on the belief that ideas for new products and services were available right there – in the heads of their employees. So the key driver behind this initiative was to empower the entrepreneurs, or to use a commonly accepted variation of the term, the "intrapreneurs" – people in the company with ideas about new products and services, to come forward and do something with their idea. The boot camps, as the name implies, were intense workshops over a timeframe of three to four months, where teams worked to develop these new ideas. At the end of the boot camp, they would pitch their ideas to a jury composed of Alcatel-Lucent Belgium executives. The team, or teams, who convinced the jury would be given the go-ahead to build their idea into an actual product. This could result in the creation of a new internal business unit, or could even result in the creation of a spin-off company.

Guido told me that the key driver of this idea, the person who was pushing for these boot camps was, perhaps surprisingly, the CEO. He explained his thought process.

Prior to the boot camps, there was a tradition that the CEO would award, once a year, a prize to an employee who showed the most initiative and ideas. One year, they had a brand new car as the prize, and the car was displayed in the lobby of the company, so that people knew what was there to be won. Eventually, there was a happy winner, who drove the car away. The first thing the winner did was to sell the car, because he lived quite close to the campus and didn't need one. So, as Guido was telling me, they learned several things. First that by giving the car away, they made only one person happy. Next, even for that person, the incentive was not the right one. Following this, the CEO and Guido re-adjusted the program to become the boot camps, involving as many people as necessary. One of the very few rules for the boot camps, as it happens, is that only teams could participate.

Guido lit up several bulbs – inspiration moments – in my mind.

The first was the concept of "open innovation" – the idea that many people in your company have ideas, not only those in the labs or product management. In fact, as I would learn from another speaker at the same conference where I met Guido, some companies such as P&G have pushed this concept of "open innovation" even further, crowd-sourcing ideas from employees, clients, partners, families of employees or even the general public.

The second bulb was about the role of the innovation team – it should be about enabling other people to do innovation, not about doing innovation themselves. This indeed was the big mistake in the "black ops" initial approach – the rest of the employees had the mistaken impression that it was only possible to innovate if you were in the innovation team. It turned out to be counter-productive to the objective of making the company more innovative.

The third bulb was the use of the word "entrepreneur" or the "intrapreneur" variation to denote some of our employees.

Inspired by these findings, the team set out to create "Innovation Challenges" at SWIFT, to engage all the employees in giving their ideas about how to innovate products, services and process. It turned out to be a big success (more on this later).

The team figured that if Innovation Challenges were such a success at SWIFT, there should be a way to run something similar for our community of clients and partners. The idea of running a challenge with the community was born. Now, we thought, where is the place where community meets? Of course, all of us thought about Sibos – the annual conference organised by SWIFT for the financial community. So, we narrowed it down to running an innovation challenge for Sibos participants. The next Sibos was in Hong Kong in September 2009.

There was an additional detail – how to sell to those within SWIFT who were organising Sibos that we should have an innovation challenge as a special feature.

We started to brainstorm about the name we would give to the challenge. I seem to recall that the fact I spent eight years of my life in Burundi in Africa probably had something to do with it. At some point, the name emerged.

Innotribe.

It was a stroke of group genius.

A name that combined all the values we wanted.

- Innovation.
- The tribal aspect of open innovation.
- Simplicity and authenticity.

There it was.

The Innotribe logo (copyright SWIFT)

PART 3
ENGAGING IN INNOVATION

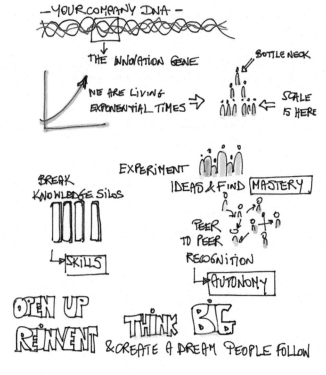

"If you want to build a ship, don't herd people together to collect wood and don't assign them tasks and work, but rather teach them to long for the endless immensity of the sea."
(ANTOINE DE SAINT-EXUPÉRY)

THE RECIPE for enabling innovation in an established company has many ingredients.

I have no evidence that all of these ingredients are necessary or indeed sufficient.

I can only tell you that the combination of these ingredients has transformed many of the companies and industries that I have observed.

In cooking, each chef has his or her own twist in making a dish. In the same way, I think that these ingredients will need to be combined in ways that fit the culture of where you are.

So here, dear chef, are the key ingredients and the recipe. Now time for you to make a dish in your own restaurant.

CHAPTER 14
THE PEOPLE

"Open innovation" uses the observation that many people in your company have ideas, not only the people in the labs or product management.

The innovation team should enable other people to innovate.

The innovation team is not there to innovate. Many people never get past this.

This indeed was the big mistake in the "black ops" initial approach of many companies that I have observed – employees were under the impression that it was only possible for people in the innovation team to innovate. This is counter-productive to the objective of making companies more innovative. I will go as far as to say that it's the biggest misconception about the innovation process.

Entrepreneur is a well-known word. Its variation, "intrapreneur", is less familiar. I've been thinking a lot about this word.

How do you spot and recognise an intrapreneur?

Does every company have intrapreneurs in the ranks?

You may think your intrapreneur is this:

- Young.
- Dynamic.
- Motivated.
- Energetic.
- Commercially minded, extrovert person.

He or she was the first to have the new iPhone and the first to know about Angry Birds, or something like that. They are currently telling everyone how 3D printing is going to change absolutely everything in three years time.

You probably will be wrong.

You may think you'd be able to spot one easily, among a bunch of "ordinary" people. Chances are you will not. You may think you can identify them on internal company social networks as the people generating ideas every day or week. Again, probably wrong.

Intrapreneurs come in all forms, shapes, and ages. Over time, I have observed many of them, and I think that the three qualities that define them are:

- Patience
- Perserverance
- Passion

And the good news is: you have many of them.

They are there, patiently waiting for their moment, their opportunity. Once you get them to talk about their idea, you can immediately see the spark in the eye, the passion. And you will see that once they get going, nothing will stop them.

When in the end they are identified and show themselves, you usually observe surprise – their direct manager may say – gosh, I didn't know they were so passionate on this subject!

It is sad that many of them will go unnoticed. Because, contrary to what you may think, they are not the best marketers, who will give you their pitch in the escalator and won't let you get out before they're done.

Most intrapreneurs need help to get going – coaching, protecting, nurturing. They need to understand there is an opportunity to come forward. You will need to gain their confidence. Their idea will most probably be disruptive to the immediate operation and environment; so will not necessarily be welcomed. I have seen intrapreneurs being fired.

I have noticed that intrapreneurs are less shy in the presence of someone external to the organisation. I will later discuss "brown bag" sessions, where outsiders are invited for a talk or to mingle with employees. And I have observed that intrapreneurs would use the opportunity to step up.

To the general surprise of everybody.

CHAPTER 15
COMMUNICATION

COMMUNICATION was and still is a sweet and sour topic for innovators everywhere. While innovators often shine in their wider industry, internal communication is frequently much harder.

Indeed, the one lesson I learned, and this is valid especially for R&D and innovation teams everywhere, is – when you do something, tell people what you're going to do before you do it, tell them what you're doing while you're doing it, and tell them what happened after it's been done. Don't expect people to read things on the Internet and intranets – spread the news.

It is not about the "What?" – the content. It is always about the "How?" – the style, format and spirit of communications.

The usual approach for internal communications is very much a top-down style: controlled and strongly vetted, produced only by people in the communication department, conforming to strict guidelines and templates.

But top-down does not respect the open innovation principle. In fact, open innovation only works with "bottom up" channels, notably internal social media platforms (such as Yammer or Chatter, which replicate many functions of Facebook and Twitter on internal company networks). But that is far from sufficient.

Something else that is also often neglected is the style of communications.

An engaging style:

- Emphasises personal touch rather than the professional polish. It is always better to see Matteo's handwriting or Mariela's drawings rather than Powerpoint slides.

- Emphasises people as much as ideas. Always emphasise the *tribe aspect*. For example, after an event, the first report could be a "feel good" video – a video that shows the "vibe" of the event, rather than what was said. The emphasis is on "homemade". It is preferable to have a video or a blog put together by people from the project teams rather than professional designers. While the end result may contain some amateurism, the boost to the team morale from producing it is largely worth the effort.

Finally, communication about innovation itself is a challenge.

- The first challenge is of a technical nature. Internal policies about accessing the Internet are still on the restrictive side in many companies. In my experience, this makes things just difficult enough to prevent the casual browsing of websites, Twitter feeds and YouTube videos. Of course, while employees can freely access these sites in the evenings and weekends from their homes, you cannot expect all your target audience to do so regularly. This first key challenge can be partially resolved by the iPad. I've noticed that companies are becoming more amenable to allowing access from iPads and other personal computers to the corporate wireless network.

- The second challenge is about the meaning of innovation to every employee. The questions which emerge most often are:

- "What do you do?" and
- "How is this relevant to my job?"

While you might sense these issues intuitively, you will discover more when you run an employee survey. I suggest using NPS – Net Promoter Score. The idea is to make the survey as simple as possible by asking essentially one single question – in this case something like: "Would you recommend the work of the innovation team to your colleagues?". The answer is provided on a scale from 1 to 10, 1 meaning "absolutely not", and 10 meaning "absolutely yes".

The NPS score is computed by subtracting the percentage of detractors (those who answer 1 to 6) from the score of the promoters (those who answer 9 and 10). Other answers are ignored.

Whatever your score, there are other figures that need to be looked at. The first is response rate – if people are even taking part, this indicates that they care and are engaged with innovation.

The whole point is to have an open, bottom-up ideation and involvement.

But you have to be realistic in your aims. For example if your company is going through Six Sigma or a similar efficiency improvement program, the typical employee or manager has very little time to give to activities not concerning their immediate line of work.

CHAPTER 16
ENGAGING EMPLOYEES

Do you want all of your employees to be promoters of innovation?

Alas, this is not a reasonable goal.

In fact I have confirmed with many other peer heads of innovation that this is in fact an impossible goal. There will always be people who will want to do their job and be good at it, but not necessarily innovate within it. And this is perfectly fine.

One solution is "Brown Bag" sessions, lunch-hour sessions where all the interested employees are invited. Offer a brown bag sandwich lunch to everyone coming (thus the name) so that they don't have to worry about getting lunch in a rush after the session.

Brown Bags is a quick hit, and I have observed it working in many situations and companies.

Outside of quick hits, what is really needed is a group of promoters, or using my terminology, "Megaphones".

These people will also be the innovation ambassadors in your company and amplify messages.

Open innovation works by opening the idea pipeline to anybody inside and outside the organisation. This can be done in co-creation events focused on particular topics. This can also be an unsolicited idea entered into the idea box. The latter is rare, almost non-existent in my experience. In any case, all ideas end up in the idea box.

The Megaphones take it from there.

The Megaphones connect the owners of such ideas with those people who may be interested, and monitor what happens.

It is very important for the credibility of the process to keep it transparent so that all people involved know exactly what happened. Having an idea rejected is much better than not knowing what happened to it – it's important to learn from mistakes.

It is also very important to avoid what is called the "steward syndrome" where the owner of an idea ends up not being involved after entering it into the box. The temptation of doing that is always present.

- Many people who go to the idea box will enter things such as "wouldn't it be nice to reduce our operating costs by 20%". Or, even more often, "here is an external company that has a product that we may use for such and such – can somebody get in touch and evaluate?". The people entering these ideas intend somebody else to follow up on them. This shows, in my experience, a lack of passion and commitment – in other words, a lack of entrepreneurship.
- There will also be cases where one of the Megaphones develops a liking for a particular idea, and slowly but surely, takes ownership from the idea owner to drive it forward. You can imagine what image this projects, not

only to the idea owner, but also to people watching the process – a major drop in credibility.

- Some ideas will go through this first scan by the Megaphones, and not find a fast solution (either connecting the owner with the person who can do something about it, or dropping it). The next step for these ideas is for them to be pitched to an Innovation Steering committee, as described later in the "Innovation process and the sandbox" section. The Megaphones help the idea owner to produce the pitch and also to prepare the ground for the pitch by connecting the idea owner with the relevant business people.

The constitution and composition of the Megaphone team is not an easy task. But once established Megaphones are vital in the management of open innovation.

My suggestion is to change the Megaphones every year, so that you give the opportunity to as many people as possible. This defines the Megaphone team as a virtual one, rather than a permanent body. I have seen many versions of Megaphone teams.

In some cases, people were "bombarded" (volunteered) by senior managers to be part of the team. This is not recommended, as invariably some of them will lack motivation. I have seen large teams (in excess of 15 people), where each member had about 10-15% of their time allocated to the task. Again, the success rate varied.

My recommendation is to organise recruitment fairs for the Megaphones, open to everyone, in other words, to look for motivated volunteers. This puts a heavy load on the selection process, but has the most chance of getting a motivated and powerful Megaphone team.

CHAPTER 17
THE EVENTS, INSIDE AND OUTSIDE

SOME OBSERVERS see events as a kind of "nice to have" activity.

The reality is that there is no open innovation without the events. The culture of the company cannot be changed without some clear and noticeable events to mark the change.

My colleague Mariela talked to me about a Google idea called "the summers of code".

It is an initiative focused on younger people, just out of school, giving them the opportunity to write applications and programs for various open source projects. Google gives them an overall theme, projects where they can contribute, mentorship and stipends. The overall goal is to provide these young people with an opportunity to taste real-world software development experience (and of course to hire them afterwards to work for Google).

This initiative breaks the silos of age, hierarchy and functions. I loved the "open" approach. The reason I put open in quotes is because I mean it in the "open source" context – the movement in the software engineering world where the computer code of programs and applications is public, for everyone to reuse and build upon. This approach leads to disruptive change.

My suggestion is to engage the entire company to generate ideas for innovation.

The trick is that an event, a campaign – has a beginning and an end and a clear timeline. I am also keen on campaign and competition aspects. In my mind, this inspires energy and entrepreneurship (in this case intrapreneurship).

Ideally an Innovation Challenge engages the entire company and therefore needs buy-in from senior management. But it is equally important to work out the nature of the prize, and how should people enter the competition, as teams or as individuals?

Best practice companies will respond to this by opening the competition only to teams (a team being a minimum of two persons). Should participants obtain some company time to work on their proposals? This is controversial but my suggestion is that employees work in their own time on their ideas. It's important to have passionate people on board. And passionate people don't count the time.

What should the prize be? Don't belittle the accomplishments with "gadget prizes" (iPods, etc). The prize for the winning team will be to implement their idea on the company's time and money.

As an example, one of the big successes I had was organising a competition aimed at improving document reviews.

The daily life of many people is writing and reviewing documents other people have written. In this example, this process reflected the functional silos of the company, whereby these documents were considered literally as contracts between functional units and were thus heavily reviewed, almost in the way that lawyers would review legal material. Both the process and the technology sustaining the process (exchanging documents by email) needed upgrading.

The employees of this company were challenged to provide ideas to innovate this whole cumbersome process. And it was a big success. In terms of attendance, about 10% of the company participated. People outside of the teams were providing help – for example a system admin who made available a testbed with temporarily unused computers and software for the teams to use. It had global coverage and multi-disciplinary teams. It had enthusiasm and energy. It had buzz.

The winning team pitched the use of Wiki-inspired technology and tools to enable collaborative document review in the company.

And they got to do it. It is very important to follow the challenge with the actual implementation of the winning idea – this time using company time and resources. This nurtures the entire challenge idea with credibility – you need to show you "walk the talk".

After successfully spreading innovation in the company, the next step is to focus on the industry around the company. This is the next natural step of open innovation.

It is a strategy often used by innovators – light the fire outside, and let it spread back to you.

It's surprisingly effective – an idea or a proposal has a better chance of being accepted if it comes from outside than if pitched by an insider.

So if the innovation challenges have successfully engaged your employees, then try to engage your customers, partners and other key stakeholders in external open innovation events.

But it is important to invest in time and effort to make these events engaging and exciting so that your people actually want to come and give you their ideas.

Time for a quick inspirational detour – let's look at a couple of case studies.

The Value Web is an interesting company.

As the name implies, it is a network of practitioners in the design and facilitation of human interactions. They focus on collaborative problem-solving. Also interesting is their structure – each member has his or her own company and endeavours, and the members regroup occasionally for specific events. They also have developed a technique for visual representation and summary of these collaborative sessions, called "scribing". The scribes produce very colourful and beautiful drawings, on Value Web's trademark rolling whiteboards. It is a very powerful technique for summarising, especially because these pictures are memorable and are good to bring back and hang on office walls to act as reminders for a long time about the discussion that took place.

Innotribe is another good case study on how to do open innovation events, with very strong differentiators.

The first key differentiator is the visual identity. Over time, Innotribe has developed a very strong visual identity that is an integral part of the brand.

The second differentiator is the type of people brought to "ignite" the groups.

They are not called speakers, because their job is to help facilitate and co-create ideas with the people who choose to join the Innotribe sessions. It is important to have a wide representation of people and not the "usual suspects". Gen-Y, philosophers, technology evangelists, venture capitalists, futurists and forward thinkers have at one point or other ignited Innotribe events.

The third differentiator is the format. An Innotribe event is a happening.

For the participants, the fourth differentiator is a mix of inspiration and learning from the Igniters, playing with the other participants in activities to practice what was learned, and co-creating ideas in interactive workshops.

The fifth differentiator is the challenge. There is always a sense of competition, so that teams composed of perfect strangers on day one end up being part of a two or three-day team, ready to win.

The sixth differentiator is the topics. They need to be motivational and inspirational, in the sense that people will be encouraged to think hard and meaningfully and look to the future. Over time, Innotribe advanced from the technology "safe" subjects and moved into new domains, such as new corporate organisations and cultures, new economies, banks for a better world and others. All these factors encourage the creation of a tribe – essentially a bond that transcends the event and establishes a longer-term relationship.

Below are reproductions of several reports and blogs of Innotribe events, illustrating these differentiators.

Corporate Culture session summary – Innotribe@ Sibos Toronto 2011

For the first time we tried some topics that were not technical, but rather philosophical. But that doesn't mean that the issues discussed aren't at the heart of the way we do business, on the contrary.

There were 3 chapters in this session:

- Structure.
- Leadership.
- Personal Behaviour.

Mark Dowds (CEO, Brainpark) introduced us to two 'disruptors of the peace': Stowe Boyd and Harold Jarche, who explored the history of hierarchical structures in companies and how technology and the media at large influences corporate structures.

Mark started with a quote from Winston Churchill: "First we shape our buildings, then they shape us", which got picked up by Stowe Boyd (Web Anthropologist and Edgling) who altered it to "Media shape us. We make our tools, and they shape us".

Harold Jarche (Principal, Life in Perpetual Beta) then quickly described our society as 'layered', he sees four layers: Tribal – Institutional – Markets – Networks, which currently exist at the same time. He asked the question if there is tension between those four layers, and whether that tension is positive or not?

Then Sean Park (Managing Director & Founder, Anthemis Group) talked us through a new, plausible model for a corporate organisation, referring to a TED talk from Geoffrey West on the scalability of cities. Sean's business model aims to resemble more a city than an army, called an Anthemis structure. In this model, the company is no longer at the centre of the world, but rather a part of a larger, inter-connected, resilient structure, and the first rule for doing business is "do no harm".

This led perfectly into 'streetwiZe'. In a short movie clip we were confronted with the harsh reality of people who have to survive on the streets every day. They have developed something called 'street skills', a set of skills that can be beneficial in our corporate world as well. There are lessons to be learned from those people, or as Jerry Michalski tweeted "we so under-estimate the poor" (@jerrymichalski)

Laura Merling, (SVP Application Enablement Business Unit at Alcatel-Lucent) showed us a video to illustrate the fact that failure is essential for success. The recipe consists of several ingredients, the first one being a clear and daunting mission like "Save the whales" sort of, or 'Innovate the financial busi-ness'. Another ingredient is the team: a bunch of different people, with different skills, chosen and selected with care. Adding to the flavour is 'Motivation'! Keep your people inspired and motivated in spite of the hurdles of working towards that daunting goal. And finally: celebrate your successes!

Dan Marovitz (Managing Director, Buzzumi) stated that "the past tends to persist", what he meant by that is that the way we do things today, is probably the way things will be done tomor-row, in spite of new technologies or insights that would enable us to do things differently!

He used the United States' Electoral College to illustrate his point. He explained that it was a great solution to a problem back in the 18th century. While, society and technology have evolved significantly since then, still the president of the USA will be elected by this historical mechanism: the Electoral College. His final point was that it takes "a decisive action and a choice", or persistence and courage, to make change happen.

Tom LaForge (Global Director of Human and Cultural Insights, The Coca-Cola Company) explained that the innova-tive mindset requires us to do things, to behave in a way that initially was not requested from us. And those corporate struc-tures should adapt to these new behaviours in order to benefit from the emerging activities. "Be really good at what comput-ers can't do" was his last piece of advice.

TA Mitchell (Founding Partner and Director, Co Company Ltd.) investigated the kind of behaviour that makes us successful in our careers, and how it used to be around four domains:

Credibility – Energy – Reach – Impact and Influence.

But now, with the Internet at our fingertips, people can rapidly expand their reach, build their credibility and raise their impact.

This constantly and rapidly changing environment requires us to adopt a 'learner mentality', as opposed to a 'learned mentality'.

Innotribe Bangkok: Enter your hyper-connected future

It is almost paradoxical that, in this increasingly connected world, meeting people 'in reality' becomes more and more important.

As Jennifer Sertl (@jennifersertl) told me at our Innotribe@ Bangkok event: we've been Twitter friends, but now, after this event, I feel part of the tribe. Jennifer has captured, very elegantly, the key reason we produce these events- to establish a deep, personal connection with a particular topic and the people interested by that topic.

The Innotribe@Bangkok event was about the hyper-connected corporation of tomorrow. William Saito (@whsaito) started the event. An entrepreneur at heart, a venture capitalist, advisor to various national governments around the globe, William explained some basic ingredients for innovation in Asia and elsewhere – all these very dear to my heart as well – passionate teams, new market opportunities being opened by technology and connectivity, the eternal dilemma of failure versus the need to innovate. In short, there is no standing still – we need to move.

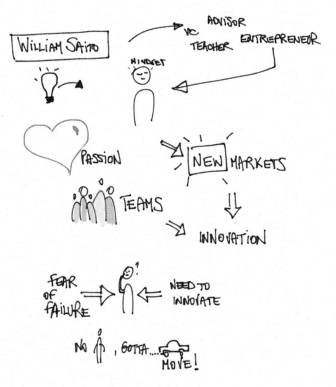

The hyper-connectivity topic was framed by Guibert Englebienne (@guibert) of Globant – we live in exponential times and corporations can't afford to have hierarchies and structure that prevent scale. And to prove the point, Globant, the company he co-founded, is growing at an incredible rate (from 70 people in 2004, to 2500 in 2011), out of their head-quarters in Buenos Aires, Argentina.

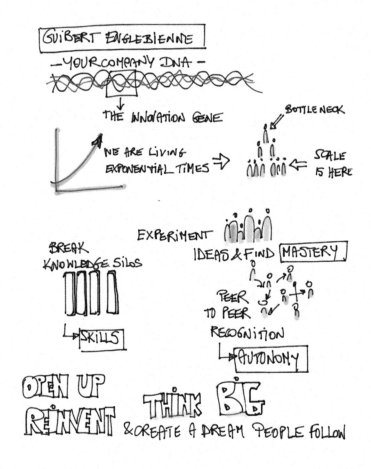

Mark Pesce (@mpesce) illustrated how the increase in connectivity drives self-regulation and self-organisation. He used Uber as an example. This is a Smartphone app which links a person in need of transportation and a nearby participating taxi driver (it is available in the San Francisco Bay Area, and spreading). Seems simple? Yes, and it is disrupting a whole industry, because it is removing friction – something that prevents scaling. In this case, the cab companies with their central dispatching.

Peter Vander Auwera (@petervan) of Innotribe introduced another important concept – the API (application programming interface).

The technologists reading this will know what the term means – it comes from computer science, and denotes how to access a piece of functionality. You don't need to know how the function is performed; you just need to know how to access it to get the work done. Translated to a hyper-connected business, it means providing – openly – access to your core business functions. Why should your company do that? To remove friction, and increase transaction flow. The friction in this case is providing the interface to your business yourself – you have to cover all different needs and combinations. Providing an API allows many more people to do that, including those who know best what they need – your customers.

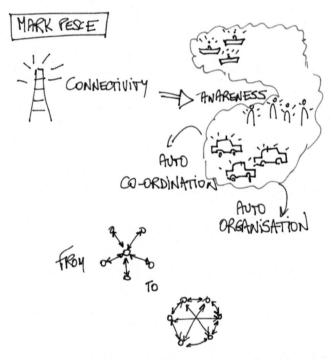

Of course, open doesn't mean without control. Peter talked about other important topics for the hyper-connected economy – digital identity and digital asset management. How to identify securely who accesses your APIs and how the information (digital assets) flows securely from user to user? These are the subjects of an Innotribe incubator project called the "Digital Asset Grid". We all thought about the implications of hyper-connectivity, frictionless and scalable organisations and APIs. How do we know a company shows signs of being hyper-connected? What are the barriers to reaching this goal?

Eiji Hagiwara, vice president of the IT services division of Mitsui & Co. and Luc Meurant (@lucmeurant), head of

Banking at SWIFT, illustrated some of these questions using the aviation industry as a metaphor, picking up on the exponential growth Guibert talked about – just think of the increase in the complexity of airplanes and air networks in the last 50 years.

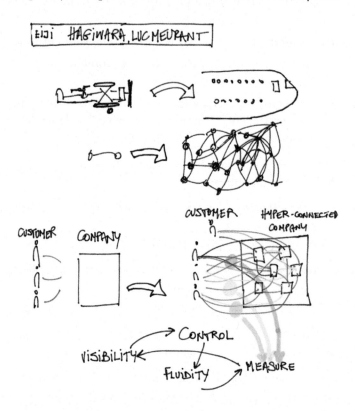

Here is what the group has identified as hyper-connectivity Key Performance Indicators (KPIs). Here's your own lab, dear reader: assess your company along these KPIs.

- Situational awareness – is every employee of your company aware in detail of the organisation? For example, peers with similar interests.

Reputation – how do your customers rate you, out there on social media for example? How is your Wikipedia entry?

- Customer satisfaction – do you have difficulty in scaling your scanning of all the information feeds? Are your employees empowered to scan?
- Adoption rate – how easy is it to become your customer?
- Openness – how easy can customers combine your services with others?
- Connectedness – how many touch points do you have with your clients? The more you have, the less friction you will have.

And here are some barriers to hyper-connectivity that Mark and the group identified:

- Time – If it were done when it were done, twere well done quickly;
- Territory – you can't be everywhere at once;
- Talent – some people are naturally better at it than others;
- Trust – must exist for commerce to succeed;
- Tongue – language barriers persist until we all speak Globish;
- Tension – frictions in teams between humans.

How do people behave, communicate in hyper-connected companies? What tools will be available for them? How do you gauge your organisation's fitness?

Jennifer Sertl (@jennifersertl) establishes the deep behaviour, the soul of the hyper-connected company, as having employees who:

- are resilient – learn from failures (which implies that an organisation should not be afraid of failing);

- are responsive – sensing and scanning accurately the environment;
- reflect – having the ability and time for deep thinking.

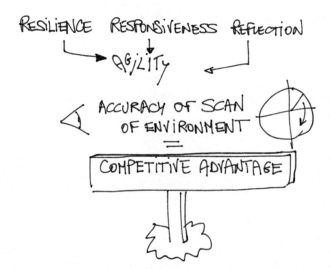

This will build agile companies, with competitive advantage.

Dan Marovitz (@marovdan), founder of Buzzumi, and Matt McDougall (@sinotechian) of SinoTech Group surprised everyone with some simple observations, such as: "how come companies producing knowledge – such as consultancies – struggle to deliver their goods virtually?" We think we're equipped but the hyper-connected corporations will need more, many more tools. The Office suite of tomorrow will be composed of directory, scheduling, messaging, payments, workflow, analytics, search and communication. Dan is a regular Innotribe "Igniter". He was head of product management at Deutsche Bank prior to starting Buzzumi, a knowledge sharing platform.

There you go – I hope you have been ignited by the hyperconnected future as I have been.

(cartoon by Hugh MacLeod @gapingvoid)

What's the next big thing in banking? Ask Innotribe

The next 'dangerous sea of disruption' is being explored by Fidor Bank in Germany.

Matthias Kröner, the CEO of Fidor, and Chris Skinner, the CEO of Balatro (and, incidentally, agitator-in-residence at Innotribe) looked at linking traditional banking and social networks. The key disruption here is the customer on-boarding model: you can register as a client with your Facebook account, or you can get authorised by sending in some documents or affiliations (such as another bank account), or go through a full "know your customer" process. A different level of products and services corresponds to each of these. In addition, the bank provides aggregated views of accounts and various holdings, in a super-simple intuitive interface. I like what Matthias said: "there is no law that says that banking transactions must be boring".

Fidor Bank – innovation, social media, simplicity

Matthias was also very amusing. For example he mentioned he worked in restaurants, and that if restaurants had the same opening hours as banks, they would open at 3pm, to allow their employees to have proper lunch. This has a ring of truth…

Which brought us to the next sea of change, in customer service.

Anthony Thomson, chair of Metrobank entertained us about how, in this increasingly virtual world, it is important to establish a personal touch with your employees and customers. Metrobank is big on establishing branches, which they call "stores", that are totally different. The staff is hired for their communications ability (and smiling!). They want to have fans and not customers.

Metrobank, the bank who has fans, not customers

We then explored another deep sea with Laura Merling, VP for development platforms at Alcatel Lucent – technology changes and players. There are a lot of things to say, but I think I managed to capture this in a very easy to understand drawing:

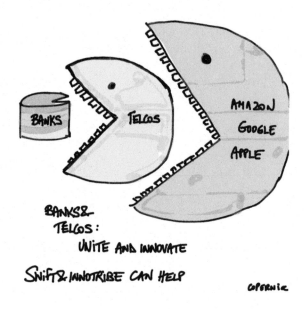

The eco-system in mobile payments

PART 4
BRINGING INNOVATION TO REALITY

'And so castles made of sand, fall in the sea, eventually'
Jimi Hendrix

THE LAST PART emphasised the recipe for engaging your employees and stakeholders in open innovation. The end result of this is ideas.

The next step is bringing these ideas to life.

CHAPTER 18
THE PROBLEM INNOVATORS ARE FACING IN ESTABLISHED COMPANIES

WHEN YOU COME BACK with the co-created ideas and pitch them to the market and product managers "back home", you will get at best a "nice idea, but I have no budget to do anything with it" answer, and at worst "please don't bother me with this stuff".

The other major problem is the way budgeting is done in established companies – the budgets usually are totally allocated with zero slack for taking up anything new and unforeseen.

In many companies, the budget process for any particular year starts by mid-year in the previous year.

It involves an elaborate process of collecting the input from the regions and markets. This typically results in "demand" that is much higher than the "supply" available. The "supply" of resources is separately decided by the CFO based on economic forecasts. The various parties then engage in a negotiation to bring down the demand to pretty much exactly the level of the supply. In fact this is a well-oiled process, attuned to optimising the operating costs, renewing and maintaining the infrastructure and products, and incremental functional releases of products and services. Unfortunately it does not work well for exploring and trying new ideas – there is no slack for this.

This is very visible with respect to mobilising operational and development resources such as IT and support. But it has more subtle repercussions as well, and extends into front-end processes such as marketing and selling.

The budgeting process also covers the commercial revenues – and is based on economic forecasts and, perhaps more importantly on the sales and revenues forecasts that the regions provide. The budgeting process is frequently a negotiation between the regional management and the marketing management. This results in sales targets being set for the year ahead, which then trickle down to individual objectives within the region. Again, a well-oiled process, but it does imply that any new product or service or initiative that was not forecasted in the budget will get, at the very best, minimal attention in the region.

So, this is a very existential question – if open innovation is good at generating ideas but has no means to put them into practice, what is the value of it?

All innovators will face this moment of profound doubt. And what they will quickly realise is the need for a space where innovation can happen without impacting the core business and where people have time to work on new ideas.

When facing the same problem, one source of inspiration for my team and me was Chris Wasden, head of the innovation practice for healthcare at PWC. Chris was an entrepreneur in a previous life, and in touch with innovation in one of the most innovative industries.

The idea that I was pursing until then was essentially about making some of the clients of my company co-invest in a shared innovation utility.

Chris didn't really believe that money was the solution. His point was that resources and time were the problem and we needed to provide for these. Chris then explained his framework for innovation management – idea generation and management, idea incubation, product acceleration and product scaling.

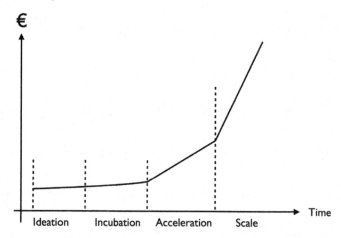

Innovation Management framework from Chris Wasden

The next step is to design a framework for progressing these ideas.

What Chris advised is to focus on the idea incubation piece.

CHAPTER 19
BUILDING A SANDBOX

LET'S FIRST better understand what an incubator is by using a metaphor.

Core business: a castle with thick walls

Consider the core business of your well established company as "the castle".

The castle is solid, with thick walls, long-lived.

As is your core business.

But the castle is not very agile.

The goal of the people in the castle is to make sure the castle serves its purpose – they are focused on optimising, not innovating.

What do you think happens to this person when she talks to the people in the castle?

The entrepreneur with an idea

Usually, the castle people will not be very friendly to this person. In fact – the more her idea is disruptive the more unfriendly they will be.

They might pour burning oil on her!

So, if the castle is not the most suitable place for innovation, where should it be? If you go back to when you were a child, where was it that you could play, experiment and do all sorts of crazy things?

The sandbox: the place to experiment

The sandbox of course!

The sandbox is an "incubator" – a protected place where people with ideas can "play", or to try out their ideas, without impacting the castle. Very much like the sandboxes of our childhoods. The incubator is the place where you can try, experiment, fail, try again, fail again, and eventually learn and succeed. The key ingredients for innovation.

CHAPTER 20
MAKING THE SANDBOX
WORK FOR YOU

So Chris' idea was to focus on the incubator. His rationale was that this is, in the big picture, the easiest way to progress, as it implies convincing only the management. This requires some clarification.

I mentioned the idea of a shared incubation utility. The idea was one way to provide the funds missing because of the zero-slack budgeting process. The other rationale is that it would be beneficial to share some innovation ideas and efforts, in an open innovation framework, with stakeholders around the company. While Chris thought this was an excellent idea, he also said that it went too far. It is better to walk before running.

The potential pitfalls were numerous:

- Heavy contractual arrangements (legal, IP, patent, risk aspects).

- Revenue sharing and splitting arrangements from the proceedings, whether this would be open to all banks or only some, etc.

The key issue was thus governance – if someone invests in a shared utility, what do they get in return in terms of command and control?

Instead, said Chris, a simpler first step is to have your company finance the incubator, but make the incubator available for the company and in addition to the community as a shared open innovation resource.

In other words, it only requires convincing the top management of the company to allocate these funds. But it is an easier sell as the funds will actively engage external stakeholders in co-creating new products and services, something that is very appealing – it is easier to be convinced that a customer will buy a product she co-created with you than another one.

Once the funding of the incubator is, hopefully favourably, decided, the governance issue is simplified but not entirely gone. As it is financed with your money, the governance is not anymore about who benefits and controls. But the question remains – how do you decide which ideas to put in the incubator?

It appears to be a simpler problem, but it requires a careful examination of your company's decision processes.

Should you ask your board to decide? In many established companies the board is required to approve major releases and enhancements to the existing products and services. Again, this is a process attuned to evolution and optimisation, but not innovation. The process is based on the provision of detailed business cases and risk analysis – clearly not suitable for assessing early stage ideas.

Gating processes for products and services development exist in many companies and are attuned to *existing* product and service evolution. In fact the gating starts when the incubation ends – when there is a business model and potential market associated with the idea. However, the gating process mindset is to filter and reduce. The incubator focus is to enable and augment ideas, contradictory in terms of mission.

Should you ask the Executive Committee (or the CEO and his immediate reports) to decide? There are some interesting points on both sides of this question. Ultimately yes of course (remember, we are talking about a company's money). But the executives themselves may not necessarily be comfortable with this. They may not be equipped, from a subject matter expert perspective, to decide which were the best ideas from the pipeline to incubate. In other words, they need advice.

The fact is that in an open innovation context, ideas can come from anywhere, so it is clear as well that the expertise may not reside at your company. In addition, the process of decision-making requires experience, similar to that possessed by venture capitalists.

My recommendation, after having successfully tried it, is to assemble a group of people, like Chris, who will advise you about the ideas to select, and also, perhaps even more importantly, help you enable these ideas, appropriately called – the 'Enablers'.

Who you need as Enablers are:

- Recognised experts in your industry, with clear, known, strong opinions
- Experienced entrepreneurs, with experience and networks
- Observers (typically "neutral" consultants)

So these people are more than influencers, but less than decision-makers. They should look at ideas with an enabling perspective and give their opinion about how best to make them happen (and not whether these ideas should be implemented or not, this remains the domain of the decision-makers in your company). I recommend choosing these people based on their own personal achievements, and not based on "political" considerations, such as choosing them from your major clients and such.

I realise you may think I'm asking you to do an almost impossible task – gather senior, recognised people to provide advice, and for free.

You may be surprised.

Between your established company's brand, the open innovation mind-set, the power of the idea of an incubator, you will find stakeholders who will gladly help you. Why? Because by investing in your future, they ultimately invest in their own.

CHAPTER 21
(THAT DREADFUL PHRASE)
THE PROCESS

FINALLY, THOUGHT should be given to the process governing the incubator.

The process is an addition to your "traditional" product and service development process.

The idea is to embed into the process, open innovation and experimentation.

Open innovation is done by engaging the community in co-creating ideas and following through on these ideas. Some ideas will be rejected. Some "simple" ideas (quick solutions) will be immediately implemented by the relevant people, with the help of your Megaphones. Some ideas will require more thinking.

Some ideas will be "big" ones – major multi-disciplinary evolution or the creation of new process, products and services.

The "big" ideas are more complex because they imply a multi-disciplinary evolution, a new product or service, a major evolution of a product or a service, a new business model in delivering the product or service, a new process for delivery, a new pricing scheme, and a new partnering scheme.

The next step of the process for these big ideas is the pitch to an Innovation Steering Committee at your company. I suggest the Innovation Steering is a subset of the Executive Committee, ideally consisting of the CEO, CMO and the CFO. The reasons for such a senior representation are many, with the following two being the most important:

- Exposure of your intrapreneurs to the senior management.
- Avoiding the "not invented here" syndrome that may cause many ideas to be rejected by line management.

The idea owner is responsible for preparing the pitch for the steering.

The pitch, as I mentioned earlier, is very important for innovation, and you should develop coaching abilities and materials to prepare the ideas owners to pitch it well. The pitches are to be very short (10 to 15 minutes), with as few supporting materials as possible.

The pitch should talk about the 5Ws:

- "Why?" (Is this interesting for the company);
- "What?" (Is the product, service, process we are talking about);
- "When?" (Is it important to have it);
- "Who?" (Will benefit from it and with whom should we do it), and;
- "Where?" (Do we develop it – in our incubator or through someone else).?

In addition, it should spell out the "How Much?" (To get it to the accelerator stage of the process)

Guy Kawasaki, whom I respect a lot, has written a lot about how to do good pitches.

A few words on the "How Much?" question. By the nature of the incubator, the pitch is about exploring and trying – therefore it shouldn't be expected that the pitch covers detailed business cases and ROIs. This is the tricky part, especially when you have a CFO in Innovation Steering, but it should be very clear that this is what it's about. As an incubator project is deemed to be 3 to 12 months maximum elapsed time, this also limits any "pharaonic" estimates in pitches. Still, this is a tricky exercise.

The other part of the "How Much?" question is related to the "Who?" question.

One of the goals of the incubator is to allow for internal people to work on projects involving exploration and new methods/ tools/technologies.

The hope is that the internal people will go back to their usual place of work after the incubator and disseminate what they have learned. Therefore it's important to have, as far as possible, internal resources working in the incubator. To achieve that, the internal people working on the incubator should be paid for by the incubator fund, and thus the department/unit providing the people can backfill with external consultants or contractors. This can prove to be trickier than it sounds, as it could imply a lot of changes to internal accounting practices, but with patience and perseverance you should get the internal practices and policies to change to cover this aspect of the incubator.

Back to the pitch. Hearing it, the Innovation Steering may decide on one of three things:

- No thanks – they don't believe in it.
- Interesting idea, close to an existing product or service or process – proceed to the traditional development process.
- Interesting idea, proceed to the incubator.

If the idea goes to the Incubator, the next step is to pitch it to the Enablers. As the name implies, the goal of the Enablers is to look at the project with their experience and provide advice:

- About the approach to carry out the project.
- The competition.
- The potential partners.
- The scoping and cutting in steps.
- The ambition level.

While it's not in the scope of the Enablers to approve budgets, the Enablers may have opinions about the amount and the way funds are spent. I've observed, over time, some Enablers gain an ambassadorial role in their respective companies, whereby they helped certain projects in obtaining pilot participation or other involvement from their company.

After the Enablers, a number of things happen:

- The project gets on the tracking list of the Incubator program manager, the requested budget is allocated, and the project starts being tracked.
- The project gets a project manager and a go-to-market resource. This may be a single person, or maybe several depending on the size and nature of the project. At least one of these people should come from what we call "the business" – the unit that will ultimately be responsible for managing the new product/service.

- If the project needs more internal resources, the wider team and the project manager should organise an internal "recruitment fair". Following the open innovation concept, I discourage the typical approach where the same "high performer" people always do all the innovative and progressive projects. The recruitment fairs should be open to anyone at your company. For the people who apply and get selected, the back-filling needs are arranged.

The project then goes on, with the overall objective of delivering a business model and early adopter piloting. The Innovation Steering and the Enablers get periodic updates and may influence the direction in which the project goes. In many instances, I've seen projects being scoped in phases.

The next step is the end of the incubation phase. The project follows a reverse process from the approval. The enablers get the debriefing from the incubation phase and advise the Steering about the acceleration phase. The Steering will decide how to proceed, and again will have three choices:

- Stop the project. This will happen if the project doesn't deliver on the expected commercial take-up, or if the project's conclusions are way above the broader organisational remit. In some cases, other parties may be interested to carry on – your company may allow them, under specific IP arrangements, to proceed with the idea. Some projects will be stopped even before the end of the incubation phase simply because the underlying idea proved not to be a good one (for example, as judged by the early adopters and pilots).
- Bring the idea "back to the castle". The incubator has proved the business model and commercial viability of the idea and the idea is re-injected into the traditional product/service development process.

- Accelerate the idea in a different model. The idea has been proven commercially viable, but the go-to-market strategy implies a non-traditional delivery model. In that case, other models may apply.

PART 5
EXAMPLES OF SUCCESSFUL INNOVATION

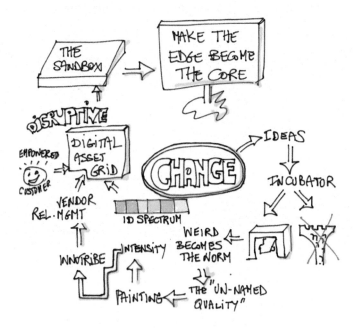

First they ignore you, then they laugh at you,
then they fight you, then you win
(MAHATMA GANDHI)

AFTER ALL THE DUST HAS SETTLED, where are the new initiatives, products and services that are coming from open innovation initiatives and processes?

It is a very significant and valid question – what is the value of innovation?

What is the value of enabling teams?

What's in it for the company and the industry?

Here I detail some of the key successes out of the innovation initiatives and projects emerging from the Innotribe incubator.

CHAPTER 22
INNOTRIBE START-UP CHALLENGES

THERE IS A THRIVING eco-system of start-ups in the financial and technology domains (called fin-tech for short) and the great majority of financial institutions do not connect at all to this eco-system.

Indeed, it's not an easy task to do so. Scouting the Silicon Valley, Singapore, Shanghai, London scenes – just to name a few – requires a network of contacts, time, resources and some form of framework of assessing all these start-ups in terms of how useful they are for one's particular business. In other words, it requires dedicated resources and effort.

Of course, dedicated resources and effort is what many institutions lack most, given their focus on reducing costs and implementing regulation.

This was a perfect opportunity for collaborative innovation led by Innotribe – connect the financial institutions to a number of quality start-ups relevant to their business. Matteo Rizzi from the Innotribe team sensed this from people he interacted with in several events. He assumed:

- The financial institutions would love it because of the very low effort to get to the start-up ecosystem. Innotribe would save costs by providing to financial institutions a quality selection of start-ups. Some institutions don't do such searches at all – this program does it for them. Some institutions do search the start-up eco-sem, at great cost – this program reduces that cost.

- The start-ups would love it because of the quick and large exposure to financial institutions (in fact, as the Pendosystems CEO would point to us – see below – it is very difficult for a start-up to pitch to large institutions because of regulation!).

To test these assumptions, Matteo pitched the concept as an Innotribe incubator project. To make things interesting and entertaining, Matteo thought the challenge would take the form of the "Dragons Den" BBC show, where candidates pitch their ideas to a jury who decide on the spot who the winner is. In the case of the start-up challenge, the jury would be composed of senior representatives from the financial industry, to whom the start-ups would pitch their wares in seven minutes maximum. To make things even more interesting, he thought about having representatives from venture capital firms acts as advisors for the start-ups, to help them refine their pitches and be able to deliver them powerfully.

The Innotribe enablers accepted the idea with cautious enthusiasm. They thought the idea was great, but that it was not really original. Indeed, there are other challenges similar to what we were proposing, not least Finovate. On the other hand, we really had an original aspect to our variation, as – contrary to others – we saw this as a public event with no participation fees. Anyway, the agreement was reached to experiment – Matteo got the go-ahead to implement a test start-up challenge at Innotribe@Sibos Toronto in 2011. Based on the feedback of this test, we would decide to continue with the program or not.

The team decided to open for start-up candidatures about two months before D-Day. Matteo was hoping to get enough of them to fill the program – he needed 15. In fact, more than 150 candidates applied! The team decided to organise an online judging round in order to reduce the number to 15. I remember being a little disturbed by the harshness of the mechanism, but indeed there was no other way.

The first start-up challenge at Innotribe@Sibos Toronto was an invitation-only session as this was an experiment. The next surprise was to see all the invited judges actually show up. The team invited quite senior people from the industry, including global CTOs to EVPs and in some case regional CEOs. All of them took the time, on a Sibos Thursday afternoon, to show up. That was already a clear indication that the event would be a success.

The event happened, the start-ups pitched, the judges judged, the advisors advised. And there were two winners! Indeed the jury couldn't decide between two finalists and decided to award two prizes of $50,000 each. It was a big hit on my budget but it was such a happening that everyone was happy and we figured we'd somehow deal with the budget later. The winners were Guardtime (www.guardtime.com. Their software produces keyless signatures to provide a provable audit trail for electronic data including proof of time, origin and integrity) and Truaxis (www.billshrink.com, a Personal Financial Management system that uses wiki intelligence to analyse credit card statements).

The incubation part of this project was to organise the first event, and assess the appetite for further events. As it was a resounding success, Innotribe has continued investing in this initiative, which is now a regular program in the financial technology industry.

Below are some blog entries explaining more about the challenges and the candidate start-ups. Also, these case studies vividly describe the entrepreneurs and the difficulties they face.

Who are the best fin-tech start-ups? Innotribe is the place to meet them.

The challenge is the place for start-ups to meet financial institutions.

I was recently speaking to a room full of people from Asian banking institutions.

I asked the room, about 150 people, "Who is in touch with start-ups in your domain?" I got three or four raised hands. There are very few touch-points between financial institutions and start-ups. Granted, a few banks do engage actively. But the majority balks at the effort and costs of exploring and understanding this thriving community. The start-ups also wonder how to get in touch with the relevant people in the institutions to pitch their products – for a start-up, access to the head of alliances or head of product management of a bank is as precious as gold.

Given our "Enable Collaborative Innovation" motto, it was quite natural for Innotribe to try and get these communities to collaborate. We organised the first challenge at Innotribe@ Sibos in Toronto in September 2011 and it was a big success. We had more than 150 start-ups apply to the challenge, a great panel of judges from the banks and venture capitalists who joined to help us select the winners. Everybody loved it. And so we decided to run the 2012 full program.

Back to Singapore.

As usual, we organised an online round of judging to get the number to 15 – 10 early stage and 5 innovators. These 15 pitched to the crowd at Plug-in@Blk71 on April 24th.

The 15 were -

- 8 Securities, www.8securities.com
- Catapult Ventures Pte Ltd, www.catapult.sg
- Clault Pte. Ltd, www.clault.com/
- Claveo Software, www.claveo.com
- DemystData, https://beta.demystdata.com
- HedgeSPA Pte. Ltd. www.hedgespa.com
- M2CASH HOLDINGS LIIMITED, www.m2cash.com
- Milaap, www.milaap.org
- Nadanu, www.nadanu.com
- NestEgg, www.nesteggwealth.com
- Pendo Systems, Inc, www.pendosystems.com
- Playmoolah, www.playmoolah.com
- PocketSmith, www.pocketsmith.com
- Tagit Pte Ltd, www.tagitmobile.com
- TalariaX Pte Ltd, www.talariax.com

An impressive list, with an incredible breadth and scope. From personal investing, to hard-core technology, to data analysis and business intelligence, to mobile payments, to cloud applications for banks. New this time, and I particularly liked that they were there, were two in what I call "Banks for a better world" category – Playmoolah (involving banks in teaching children how to invest better) and Milaap (person-to-person lending for India's working poor). I will write about "Banks for a better world", an Innotribe incubator project, later.

The morning of the event is always dedicated to rehearsals and coaching. We have several of the judges and organisers listen to the pitches, and provide advice – how to fit in the allocated time (six minutes, not one second more!), how to show passion, how to be clear.

The afternoon was for pitching to the full room – financial institution representatives, venture capitalists, journalists. They all did a great job. If you pressed me really hard to tell which pitch was best …. well, I was blown away by the pitch of Pocketsmith. Simple, powerful and clear.

After feverish counting while everybody was having drinks, the winners were announced: Playmoolah and Pendo Systems!

Taking no risk is the greatest risk of all

Playmoolah was a winner in the Innotribe Startup Challenge in Singapore earlier this year. I was inspired with what they do – a tool to help parents educate their children about the value of money – and the energy and passion of Min, so I asked her to tell her story.

Giving the floor to Min Xuan Lee (CEO and co-founder), this is what I heard:

It was an eye-opening experience to learn how different cultures use money.

Coming from Singapore to California during the height of the financial crisis, we uncovered more and more horror stories over casual conversations about debt and over-leverage, fuelled by relentless, uninformed optimism.

It was evident how this generation was fast becoming the most indebted generation in modern history. This sparked one simple question – what is the root cause of financial illiteracy in our world today?

Our curiosity led us onto a path of inquiry, into the homes of American families, volunteering to teach in public schools, and speaking to anyone who had done work even remotely related to the field of financial literacy. Over one year, we spoke to hundreds of researchers, entrepreneurs, investors, teachers, and parents. The problem was clear – children lack financial education, school intervention had not proven effective and only 32% of American parents talk to their children regularly about money.

The solutions were staring in our face. First, the problem is not simply about literacy, but in following up with real action and cultivating good habits. It's also about starting young and involving not just the child but also their parents to encourage good role models and healthy conversations about money. At the root of the problem, parents just don't know where to begin. And if the problems start at home, they need to be solved at home. But why isn't there a home-based solution to help children and parents work through money matters together?

On the other hand, children are exposed to an avalanche of mass media and games that encourage consumerism and peer comparisons of what they have, even in the virtual world. What are our kids exposed to?

While at Stanford University, we were influenced by the work of B.J. Fogg and his methods for designing persuasive technology – technology that influences behavioural change. We saw an opportunity to nip the problem in the bud and take what kids have come to love, to turn the incentives completely on their head and design good technology that inspires real-world behavioural action.

There is something powerful about an idea whose time has come. So many people rallied around the idea offering us so much encouragement and help, putting us in a position where taking no risk became the greatest risk of all. With gut indignation towards the problem, an agonising discomfort about the status quo, and the collective wisdom of all that we met along the way, PlayMoolah (http://playmoolah.com) was born.

In the PlayMoolah headquarters, there is a little desk with little chairs for the kids, filled with sketch paper and markers, Lego bricks and all sorts of toys for kids to join us in the design process. All our concepts go through prototyping and feedback from the kids before being put into production.

We design and develop play tools that put kids in the driver's seat of their own learning, empowering them with the curiosity, knowledge, skills and tools needed for financial capability. Separately, parents are provided with a dashboard where they can monitor and track their kids' progress, get involved with their kids' saving goals, or get ideas on family projects they can do at home. No other solution on the market today is tying important age-appropriate lessons about managing money to real life, real dollar and real impact.

There is a famous saying in the Valley – ask for money and you get advice, ask for advice and you get money. Through many of these unexpected conversations, we raised our seed round from a diverse group of angel investors across US and Singapore with an alignment in intention and a great humility towards something larger than ourselves. Our first investor wrote a tongue-in-cheek description on our cheque – "Pay to the Order of Play Moolah" for "Saving the world" – definitely one for the archives.

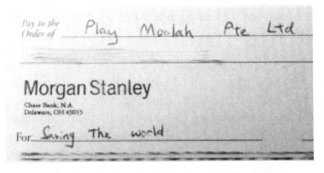

Getting investment to save the world! (Photo by Playmoolah)

We are approaching exciting times as we partner with more schools and financial institutions to offer PlayMoolah to a greater number of kids and parents around the world. As part of the International ChildFinance Movement headquartered in Amsterdam, we also hope to catalyse quality financial education and access to reach the goal of touching the lives of 10 million children around the world.

At the end of the day, we hope to inspire the next generation of young people to develop a healthy perspective of money, and to really rethink what money is. To see money as a wealth creation tool rather than an end in itself, money should serve our own dreams, personal growth and happiness. It's about enhancing the quality of our experiences, the strength of our relationships, our well-being and our health, and ultimately using money as fuel to create greater value in society. That is the true essence of start-ups that have served as a vehicle for wealth creation – because every single time we see our Playmoolah kids saving up for their goals, or giving their allowance to charity, we couldn't imagine trading what we're doing for anything else in the world.

We don't want to be too small to succeed for those too big to fail

Pendo Systems, Inc, recently won the "top innovator award" at the Innotribe Startup Challenge in Singapore. Pendo's founder is Pamela Pecs Cytron, who started her career in fin-tech at the age of 19.

The one thing we require at Innotribe is the "ASK"– what is it that the start-up is pitching for? Pam's ask was like no other, she simply said: "we don't want to be too small to succeed for those anointed too big to fail". I found the argument interesting, and the passion animating her even more. So here's her story.

Giving the floor to Pam:

I started my pitch with a timeline dating back to 1920, to the first ever Ponzi scheme, and demonstrated to the audience that as time progressed, regulations mandated that not only do the crisis we experience continue, it gets more frequent and more catastrophic each and every time.

Friday, May 18, 2012 As of 10:11 AM   New York 73°|51°

THE WALL STREET JOURNAL | MANAGEMENT

MANAGEMENT | Updated May 18, 2012, 10:11 a.m. ET

Inside J.P. Morgan's Blunder

CEO Dimon Blessed the Concept Behind Disastrous Trades; 'Blood in the Water'

On April 30, associates who were gathered in a conference room handed Mr. Dimon summaries and analyses of the losses. But there were no details about the trades themselves. "I want to see the positions!" he barked, throwing down the papers, according to attendees. "Now! I want to see everything!"

Material by Pendosystems

My theory is the centre of the universe is the position – meaning the position of an asset. The asset feeds systems in the financial eco-system. A theory supported when an article in the Wall Street Journal quoted Jamie Dimon as asking "I want to see my positions." The industry has spent billions of dollars over the past 20 years, creating new securities, building risk systems, compliance systems, flash trading but we are sending this information for processing to systems that were deployed and invented over 25 years ago. People, pivot tables and legacy applications are accounting for the world's assets. None of which drive transparency.

Her experience told her that innovation was needed in basic accounting. She left her senior position with a major technology vendor in 2005 and set out to build a global investment accounting system that would look at the world in a position-centric, multi-jurisdictional way. Pendo launched in 2007.

Pam later discovered the challenges of getting mission-critical technology adopted in major organisations. How do established companies buy from a small start-up?

Client adoption is a problem, as is accessing capital to grow. Pendo, as many other start-ups, faced the paradox: clients very favourable to the technology, but very risk averse in dealing with a start-up. Pam told me she has written to virtually every powerful person on Wall Street. She laughs when she remembers writing to Richard Branson and Donald Trump.

Back to Pam.

Since founding the company in 2007, we all have faced a world none would have imagined. In Pendo's case not only did we get hit by the financial crisis, but I battled cancer for two years. During this time, many people told me to just stop, that I'll never overcome the hurdles.

Articles in Dodd Frank now dictated that banks review their vendors for solvency. In one case I thought we got the break every start-up needs, when we were awarded a verbal agreement for a major project at one of the world's largest banks. The excitement lasted about 7 days until I was told by procurement that Pendo was too small to do business with and they could not proceed.

I did what every entrepreneur needs to do; I cut expenses, shut down payroll. Amazingly the staff all stayed to ensure the technology would not go to the shelves as too many good products do. The company was clearly facing some tough decisions and my personal capital, life insurance policy and everything I could cash in had been exhausted. But I told the staff we must keep our customers happy, our data centres running and not miss a regulatory deadline. We continue to do that.

Ask Pam about her investor experience. She prefers not to share her perspective on this, but she does say "any money is not good money".

Perseverance, passion and a lucky break make the successful entrepreneur. And patience.

The lesson we can learn from Pam is: play to win, make your mistakes fast, learn from them and move on. Reinvent but stay true to the mission and the goal. Pam says, "Close your eyes and tell me if the back office processing on Wall Street will look like it does today in 7 years?"

I wish Pam and Pendo Systems success.

Open source software for risk analytics – a valid option

Each start-up has a story to tell. As story of overcoming business difficulties, funding issues, dealing with personal hardship. A story of how passion, patience and perseverance have won over many obstacles.

So, here's the story of OpenGamma, a start-up focusing on financial risk analytics and which believes, as I profoundly do, that the open source approach to software is the most progressive and efficient approach in our hyper-connected world. I already wrote about open sourcing in the financial domain as a bold innovative move. It is also the story of three entrepreneurs who have spotted an opportunity while working in financial institutions, and decided to do something about it.

OpenGamma was one of the winners of the Belfast regional showcase of the Innotribe Startup Challenge. I've met Kirk Wylie, CEO of OpenGamma, and asked him to contribute.

Here's Kirk's story.

The idea of OpenGamma came from a need I noticed while working in risk and front office technology for financial services firms.

My job was building infrastructure for which there wasn't a viable commercial offering. With financial services firms looking for cost reductions in every part of their operations, it seemed absurd that most of their IT budget was spent on building and maintaining expensive in-house systems that didn't hold any proprietary value to the company. Trading and risk analytics systems are plumbing; as long as it works you shouldn't notice it.

So why should every firm build their own from scratch? Why shouldn't there be an open source solution out there available to all?

This thought triggered an email to the other two co-founders, and the idea for OpenGamma was born. After the credit crunch, Jim Moores, Elaine McLeod and I set out to turn our vision of a single unified platform for analytics across financial services firms into reality. We were frustrated with the state of financial technology, and we wanted to change it.

In building our flagship product, the OpenGamma Platform, we've taken all the lessons that the combined team has learned working in hedge funds and investment banks, as well as pure tech firms outside financial services.

From the very beginning, we also dedicated a lot of time to grassroots market research. We met with people in technology, on the trading and risk desks, and in senior management, to talk about their experiences with analytics and risk technology. We wanted to build something that technologists would love to deploy, end users would love to use, and procurement departments would...well, accept.

When we got to the point where we had people willing to go on record saying "If you build what you say you'll build, and you have the business model you say you will, we'd buy it", we realised it was time to start building.

Defining open source

One of the most common questions we get is: "What do you mean by open source?" We use the term open source in its full sense: all code freely downloadable online, along with full documentation, user forums, bug tracking, and so on. There aren't any catches here. To date, every component that we're legally allowed to release under an Open Source license has been.

However, although our approach is radical in the industry, our goal was never just to build open source technology. We wanted to build the best platform for financial analytics and risk management possible. We've released it under an open source license because that's what the market told us they want.

In the past, the industry has had three choices: buy a traditional, siloed trading system and spend years trying to get it to do what end users wanted; pay for an expensive, opaque external service; or build everything from scratch. With choices like that, it's no wonder the preferred choice has been to build from scratch. Over and over. Within the same firm, across firms, developers keep building the same components because vendors haven't given them what they need.

These traditional choices don't work anymore.

Of course, open source software has often been championed as the low-cost option. While it's by no means free, it allows firms to focus their IT effort on what's specific to their trading strategies, which is perhaps only 10-15% of the overall technology stack. Allowing our clients to do this type of budget optimization has been one of our main goals in building OpenGamma.

When everyone knows what's going on under the hood, users can feel confident in trusting the results that they get out of the system—and not just take a vendor's word for it.

Investors with a shared vision

We knew what we wanted to build, but we also knew it was a massive undertaking. How would we actually finance it?

While I'm generally in favour of bootstrapped business models for most start-ups these days, we knew that we were building something far too large to be done in that fashion. The sheer scope of what we needed to present as a minimum viable product meant that we needed external capital to get started.

When I first moved to the UK in 2004, I'd met with Bruce Golden and Kevin Comolli of Accel Partners. In 2009, when we decided to launch, I knew they would be perfect partners in building OpenGamma. Accel believed in our vision, we raised a Series A round from them, and Bruce joined our board.

We've since raised two additional rounds: Series B, led by FirstMark Capital in 2010, and Series C in August 2012, led by ICAP plc. Without investors who share our vision of radical disruption in the quantitative finance market, there's no way we would have been able to build a system as comprehensive as the OpenGamma Platform.

We are now moving our first customers from evaluation into full production installations. This is perhaps our most important milestone to date: some of the largest, most sophisticated capital markets participants are using our technology to manage some of the most complex derivatives portfolios in the world. Having these companies as clients is the strongest possible indication that our software works.

As with any open source project, remaining independent, and truly open, is paramount to us. Customers greatly value the neutrality and transparency that open source players contribute to the industry. We need to continue being extra vigilant not to let them down.

CHAPTER 23
BANKS FOR A BETTER WORLD

BANKS FOR A BETTER WORLD is a new trend in Innotribe topics, very much away from financial technology.

In essence, it is about:

- Bridging traditional and social finance, a kind of "fair trade" but for financial products and services.
- Connecting the unbanked, the people who are not part of the financial system because they don't have any bank relationship or account. In many developing countries, the unbanked form the majority of the people.
- Establishing a community, or movement, to influence the governments and global companies for more transparency in the way they invest.

Before we dig further, it is important to understand the genesis of this project and the people in my team who made it happen.

The originator of the idea was Peter Vander Auwera. At that time, and still today, Peter and I were following Jerry Michalski's REX (Relationship Economy Expedition) movement in San Francisco. Peter was invited to one of Jerry's famous retreats, where there was a lot of talk about abundance and trust as opposed to scarcity and stickiness. Jerry's basic point is that citizens should be able to devise an economy that is not based on scarcity (of money) but rather an abundance (of goodwill and skills that people can exchange). This was made clear to me when I went to the Share conference, which was full of such examples in the San Francisco area. Peter called it Banks for a Better World, reflecting the need for the banks (and indeed the broader financial community) to reconnect with core values.

Ashoka is a long story in itself. Ashoka supports and helps social entrepreneurs in dozens of countries. I immediately felt synergy between Ashoka and Innotribe's goals of enabling entrepreneurship (in Ashoka's case, social entrepreneurship, and in Innotribe's case intrapreneurship and entrepreneurship in the financial industry).

As is the case with serendipity, yet another important and seemingly unrelated event happened at the same time: a new member, Martine De Weirdt, joined the Innotribe team. Martine and I first connected when she was head of standards.

Over the years, Martine had been exposed, through standards and CSR involvement, to the more "remote" areas of finance, such as social finance in developing countries and topics such as "financial inclusion" – allowing as many world citizens as possible to have a bank account and thus access to financial tools.

It was therefore quite natural for her to lead the Banks for a Better World idea and start shaping it into something more.

Ashoka, were also quite curious about Innotribe. They saw in SWIFT and Innotribe a way to get in touch with the broader finance community. Also, by the very nature of Ashoka – a neutral, global not-for-profit association – they felt affinity with Innotribe at SWIFT.

Ashoka thus invited Innotribe to host a workshop at the Changemaker's week, where we floated the Banks for a Better

World idea for the first time (in addition to what we had already blogged).

What quickly became apparent, and is visualised in Mariela's drawing (that appears at the end of this book) was that:

- Banks were keen to engage in collaborative activities in order to improve their image by delivering products and services focused on developing countries and enabling entrepreneurship in these countries.
- There was a major gap between traditional finance, very well known in the developed countries, and social finance – very much unknown in developing countries with notable exceptions such as Grameen bank and their micro-credits.
- There is a lack of adequate financial instruments to support small SMEs and social enterprise, as much in developed countries as developing ones.
- There is a major issue of financial inclusion, as illustrated by India where pretty much the entire population has, or has access to, a mobile phone, but only a third of the eligible population has a bank account. The so-called "unbanked" are thus isolated from traditional financial instruments.
- Bridges between the social and traditional finance can only be established through collaborative efforts, as any single bank wouldn't have the power to resolve all these problems on their own.
- Innotribe and Ashoka could be the right "vehicle" for such collaboration.

The result of the workshop was a "manifesto" building on many of the above points.

This was very encouraging to us and fit perfectly our collaborative innovation remit. This was the first non-technology topic to become a big blob on Innotribe's radar screen. This result was also very encouraging to Ashoka.

One last thing I want to emphasise about this project is that it is neither about Corporate Social Responsibility (CSR) nor charity.

The idea is to create sustainable products, services, companies that solve problems related to "social" finance by bridging it to "traditional" finance.

The person who explains this best is Professor Muhammad Yunus, who I met at Innotribe@Sibos Osaka in 2012. Martine first met Yunus at the World Economic Forum in Davos 2012, where Innotribe was hosting a private session on Banks for a Better World. He was interested in the Innotribe approach, and eventually agreed to join the Banks for a Better World session at Innotribe@Sibos 2012 and also deliver a speech for the Sibos closing plenary.

He says that "charity money never comes back". Giving money doesn't guarantee a sustainable improvement for those receiving that money. He told me about a recent trip to Haiti, where he observed that despite massive donations and charity given since the catastrophic earthquake, the situation on the ground has improved only marginally.

His solution is the "social enterprise" – an enterprise like any other, except that the dividends are re-invested into the company. So, the mission of such social enterprises is to solve problems, and not to make money. This makes a big difference, and he has more than 60 social enterprises behind him to prove the point – notably the Grameen Bank and Grameen Danone Foods.

The focus is on long term sustainability – the initial money is invested into the enterprise not as charity, but as a means to get the social enterprise off the ground and sustaining itself.

Based on this, the following idea emerged at Innotribe@Sibos 2012: Banks for a Better World becomes a collaborative project whose goal is to create a number of social enterprises focused on bridging the traditional and social finance worlds.

The project would be co-ordinated by Innotribe, following from the collaborative innovation mission it has. The following ingredients are needed – funding, agenda setting, idea generation and, finally, creation of the social enterprises.

The banking community would provide the funding, on a voluntary basis (banks willing to participate) or a community-wide mechanism. Two ideas have been mentioned for the latter, involving SWIFT:

- Rounding the value of the payment instructions transmitted on the SWIFT network to the upper currency unit, and making the difference available to Banks for a Better World (e.g. an amount of 143,36 EUR is rounded up to 144 EUR and 0,64 EUR is kept).
- Making the SWIFT refund available for Banks for a Better World. SWIFT being a co-operative society (thus not for profit), refunds its member banks each year with any surplus income made that year.

The agenda setting for Banks for a Better World – in other words, the focus of innovation – of course will depend on the way it is funded. However, it will be important to have Enablers, people with experience on the ground such as Prof. Yunus, to drive the agenda as well.

Next is actual idea generation – spot the social entrepreneurs or start-ups who have ideas relevant to the above agenda, engage and encourage them to step forward and enable them to create solutions and social enterprises. This sounds easy, but it is not – from Innotribe's experience in the Startup Challenge, it requires an extensive network and work to produce quality ideas. In fact, inspired by the Startup Challenge, and in collaboration with Ashoka, the Banks for a Better World session gave five social start-ups the opportunity to pitch their ideas to Prof. Yunus and the other panelists. These ideas were:

- Providing young people in developing countries with financial education and bank accounts – tomorrow's future customers.

- Developing mobile banking to reach the word's unbanked communities.

- Building partnerships between specialist community lenders and mainstream banks to improve access to finance.

- Providing working capital funding to high growth SMEs and social impact organisations.

- Issuing municipal impact bonds to finance high impact social projects.

Another interesting idea came from Julius Akinyemi, a panelist in the same session. Julius is the initiator of a project called Unleashing the Wealth of Nations and a resident entrepreneur at the MIT Media Lab in Cambridge, Massachusetts. Akinyemi proposes leveraging new technology – such as the Digital Asset Grid – to create a local and nationwide "eRegistry" of all assets such as land, real property, farms and even cows and goats, that could be converted into a globally-understood and accepted common currency.

Let's see where this goes. The Innotribe team and I were tremendously encouraged by Prof. Yunus' incredible faith and drive.

CHAPTER 24
THE DIGITAL ASSET GRID (DAG)

THIS IS PROBABLY the most disruptive Innotribe incubator project at the time of writing.

Before I explain what it is, it is worth looking at the history of it and some of the key players involved. And it all comes from one of the most important subjects – Digital Identity.

The DAG is the ultimate open innovation project, hatched and co-created by numerous people in many industries.

The key figure behind the digital identity topic and ultimately the DAG, is Peter Vander Auwera. In his previous career at Microsoft, Peter was driving Microsoft's efforts to implement their technology in the context of digital identity cards in Belgium. Bill Gates declared the project a priority for Microsoft. Peter learned about all the intricacies of the subject, and, especially, met the people who mattered in the domain. One of them was Kim Cameron, then chief architect of identity. He also met Bill Gates on several occasions to report on the progress.

At Microsoft, digital identity was one of these major battles such as tablet computing. Excellent ideas that mobilised the best and the brightest and gained funding. But ultimately unsuccessful. Or, at least, unsuccessful so far.

Microsoft sensed, in late 1990's, that the topic of people's digital identity, or, more specifically, the method by which people get authenticated on the Internet, was one of the major barriers to e-commerce and to Microsoft's ambitions in this domain. Indeed, Kim Cameron got the job of Chief Architect for Identity and over time co-invented some of the key principles and methods, which are still as valid today as then. So Microsoft were the thought leaders, and of course wanted to create new products and services. The product that hit the market was called Passport – essentially providing a single sign-on to participating web sites through a single, Microsoft managed, identity (and associated email account). The initiative didn't have the expected success. One of its descendants still lives today, under another name. But clearly the viral, massive customer pickup didn't happen.

Meanwhile, the Belgian electronic identity initiative was deployed, also with less than expected fallout for Microsoft. Peter joined my team at SWIFT from Microsoft and we went on, in the first phase of the innovation team history, to implement the Lite and Integrator products.

When Peter changed roles in the innovation team to become the network builder and curator of Innotribe@Sibos, one of his areas of exploration was of course digital identity. Peter recognised immediately that while the subject remained of paramount importance to e-commerce, there was still no industry-wide initiative to solve this problem.

The tribe was interpreting the lack of success of Microsoft in rolling out an industry-wide infrastructure as essentially due to a lack of trust. While most people would trust Microsoft to provide the technology for it (in the same way that hundreds of millions of people use Microsoft Office), the picture looked different when talking about entrusting to them core digital and personal information.

Who, then, would people trust? If SWIFT's core values are standards, security and reliability, and if SWIFT is a neutral co-operative owned by the world's banks, wouldn't SWIFT be the right entity to drive this forward?

I do remember some cold sweat running down my spine – this was big, very big. Much bigger than our current scope. Peter and I went back to Belgium and thought about how to possibly move such a bold project forward.

Of course, we thought about the incubator – shaping and scoping a global digital identity infrastructure is a perfect candidate for incubation. Rather than try to cut the project in small steps to make it more acceptable, we took the opposite stance and pitched the strategic long term implications. The debate in our Innovation Steering and Innotribe Enablers was probably the most difficult one ever – of course, there was a valid concern of the project trying to "boil the ocean". In the end, everyone agreed that it was a domain worth exploring. The pitch was for two major phases – research and formulation of business scenarios, followed by a prototype implementation with some very early adopters.

Peter engaged the tribe in the research project. It was an incredible ride, with so many powerful minds looking at the digital identity topic from many different angles, sometimes in the nitty-gritty of protocols such as OpenID, sometimes bordering on the nearly philosophical discussions of whether a single identity is necessary on the Internet – or should everyone have as many digital personas as they like.

What fascinated me also was that Peter Vander Auwera could gather such a passionate support from these people, who, barely months before, were probably looking at SWIFT as some kind of a bureaucratic outfit administering BIC codes. I felt very proud that Peter and Innotribe achieved this.

What emerged from the research was in fact different from the digital identity topic that it started with. In fact, digital identity was just a symptom of a deeper issue. The issue of data, its ownership and distribution. What the team called "digital assets". And they postulated that what was indeed needed was an infrastructure to store and share digital assets. They called it the "Digital Asset Grid".

Here is how they explain it.

Imagine a new economy where the customer is fully empowered. What would it look like? What would the role of the banks be? What would be the role of infrastructure providers such as SWIFT, telcos and social networks?

Say you want to buy a car. Today, you would have to consult many web sites, visit garages, spend considerable time comparing the offers, spend energy and nerves negotiating, dealing with insurance, on and on.

In the new – digital – economy, you would be empowered: if you have a good online reputation and if your willingness to buy a car was certified (say, by a bank), then you will be simply able to state the type of car you want to buy and all the vendors would propose their best offers to you.

Doc Searls, a long-time advocate of the open source movement, author of the "Cluetrain Manifesto" and most recently of "The Intention Economy: When Customers Take Charge", calls this VRM – Vendor Relationship Management. It is defined somewhat by opposition to CRM – Customer Relationship Management. Indeed, in today's economy, you as a person, or an SME, or a company, are being CRM-ed by all the vendors you deal with.

Imagine another aspect of this new digital economy: putting a value on intangible pieces of data. Things such as your reputation on eBay, or your purchase history on Amazon. Obviously these "digital assets" have considerable value in your eyes, and also in the eyes of people buying from you, selling to you, or otherwise interacting with you. And these are only examples – digital identity information, physical or IP addresses, credit card numbers, phone numbers, health records, bank account transaction logs are other examples of digital assets.

Today, these digital assets are locked away in digital silos, with very little control about how they are managed, where they are stored, and who accesses them. Indeed, your eBay reputation is fine as long as you're buying on eBay, but what about when you're buying on Amazon? So, where's the control you're rightly expecting to have on these assets? Also, lots of people and companies are making money by selling these digital assets – are you seeing any value being returned to you, the owner?

This is what Innotribe's Digital Asset Grid project is all about – providing an infrastructure where digital assets can be stored, managed and accessed in a way that preserves the ownership, allows user empowerment and enables sharing and monetisation of these assets.

As Jennifer Schenker of Informilo puts it in her article about the Digital Asset Grid: 'Data is becoming a new type of raw material that's on par with capital and labour, according to a 2011 World Economic Forum report entitled "Personal Data: The Emergence of a New Asset Class." A handful of the largest Internet companies, such as Google and Facebook, are reaping most of the profits from collecting, aggregating, analysing and monetising personal data. But consumers have no control over and little knowledge of what is being done with their data.'

The Digital Asset Grid is composed of:

- Digital asset accounts or vaults where users (people or legal entities) load their digital assets of value.
- Infrastructure to find digital assets on the grid, and to verify that the assets are allowed to be accessed and used in the desired way.
- A marketplace where digital assets can be traded in various applications (such as buying cars).

Because the bottom line is about sharing and using value, the Grid must be highly secure and reliable, neutral, and trusted by all parties. This is the reason why the project is being researched in the Innotribe incubator. The vision is that the financial institutions could provide new digital asset management products and services to support the digital economy, and that SWIFT with other technology providers could provide and run the neutral, secure and standardised infrastructure linking the financial institutions and the users. The expectation is that SWIFT would bring the neutrality that other past and current commercial ventures lack.

The trust aspect of the digital economy will need special attention, as it cannot be replicated from today's bricks & mortar framework based on "know your customer" processes. It is envisioned that a new digital trust framework will be built on a peer-to-peer vouching system, not unlike the reputation system on eBay but open and inter-operable between all applications on the Grid. One such framework is being experimented with today in Connect.me, a social discovery network available in beta. The founder of Connect.me, Drummond Reed, is a key advisor in the Digital Asset Grid project.

Finally, the business model needs to be invented. From the empowered users who can monetise the use of their digital assets, to financial institutions who manage the assets, to vendors who have visibility to more business opportunities –

each player in the eco-system will need to find their own way to thrive. The Digital Asset Grid incubator project is testing and experimenting with these potential roles.

The Digital Aset Grid represents an opportunity for the financial industry to innovate in the fast moving technology landscape, and establish thought leadership and first mover advantage in the new digital economy.

The first part of the project, the research, changed the scope from Digital Identity – the way people are authenticated on the Internet – to the Digital Asset Grid – the way people manage and share their digital assets, including assets related to their digital identities.

Per the Incubator process, Peter Vander Auwera presented the DAG to the Innovation Steering at SWIFT and the Innotribe Enablers, with a view also of kicking off the second part of the project, the prototype. This time around, the feedback was not any more about trying to "boil the ocean", and the second phase was easily approved. The concern this time around was more about whether SWIFT should be the key driver of the DAG, as the scope of it is much bigger than the scope of SWIFT. The second phase was thus approved with this particular concern in mind, and indeed the next step is to identify other industry players to co-invest intellectual power and financial resources.

The DAG book is far from closed. Maybe you will read it again in a year or two!

One last thing I want to mention about the DAG – the disruptive nature of the project is a tribute to SWIFT and the Innotribe Enablers. They didn't shy from it – they truly embraced 'The Castle and The Sandbox', and they understood that we should have many aspects in our incubator sandbox, up to and including very disruptive ones.

PART 6
CONCLUSIONS AND RECOMMENDATIONS

Do or do not. There is no try.
(YODA)

INNOVATION is a necessary component of any established company.

Innovation is not only about invention and creativity. It is about bringing invention to concrete, measurable fruition.

There are a variety of types of innovation, including:

- **Business model innovation:** Involves changing the way business is done in terms of capturing value.
- **Marketing innovation:** Is the development of new marketing methods with improvement in product design or packaging, product promotion or pricing.
- **Organisational innovation:** Involves the creation or alteration of business structures, practices, and models, and may therefore include process, marketing and business model innovation.

- **Process innovation:** Involves the implementation of a new or significantly improved production or delivery method.

- **Product innovation:** Involves the introduction of a new good or service that is new or substantially improved.

- **Service innovation:** Is similar to product innovation except that the innovation relates to services rather than to products.

- **Supply chain innovation:** Where innovations occur in the sourcing of input products from suppliers and the delivery of output products to customers.

(thank you Wikipedia)

In the end, there is no small or big, incremental or disruptive innovation. Instead, innovation management, similarly to investment management, should manage a portfolio of all such innovations.

Enabling innovation means identifying the people – the entrepreneurs and intrapreneurs – in or around your company, who have ideas and who are passionate to do something about these ideas.

Seeking out, engaging and nurturing these entrepreneurs is open innovation.

Enabling innovation means:

- Making innovation management a function in your organisation, given to a small but passionate and motivated team, and supported by the executive. The mission of this team is not to do the innovation, but to enable it- provide support and tools to the entrepreneurs in your company and around it.

- Establishing a framework and tools that encourage social media inspired communications in your company, which will break naturally the functional and structural silos.
- Engaging your employees, clients and partners in open innovation events, with the goal of generating innovative ideas.

Once people are engaged and ideas are flowing, it is important to act and actively progress them.

This means:

- Establishing an incubation "sandbox", where ideas can be tried and experimented without risk to your core "castle" business.
- Allocating funds to the incubator, making sure there are budgets for innovation and experimentation.
- Establishing an internal process for managing the incubator, separate from the traditional development process.
- Gathering recognised and experimented "enablers" from the industry, to advise and connect your entrepreneurs to the external world.

The successful combination of all these recommendations to deliver a culture change in your company, and ultimately resulting in the profound change of inside and outside perception of your company, is no small endeavour. It requires passion, perseverance and patience. Culture and perception are the most difficult to change. At the same time, changing them is the best way to ensure long term continued success for your company.

Now what – starting, scanning, understanding the big picture?

Congratulations you've come to the end of the book, now what?

You might revisit the earlier case study on the NHS, and think how you might bring open innovation to it.

Or …

I have a personal KPI – a week without a contact with somebody outside my company is a lost week.

I call it reaching out and scanning. Building your radar screen about what matters to your company. In fact, deep down, it is just curiosity.

I cannot emphasise enough the importance of doing this. If you, personally, cannot do it because you lack time or energy, make sure you find or hire somebody who can.

Here is how I have built a deep understanding of the changes in the industry I'm working in, and some of the key people who helped.

In a nutshell –

- There are observable symptoms of a major transformation.
- These symptoms are manifestations of a deep technological change happening right now – the digitization of everything: from pictures (jpegs), music (mp3) to our digital personas and ultimately the economy itself.
- This transformation is a major opportunity for banks and others to provide new products and services to the hyper-connected generation coming to the market as employees and consumers.

I call it the "essence" of innovation in technology.

Here are many of the key igniters of this vision –

- Peter Hinssen, and his idea of the New Normal, that we are halfway through the digital revolution. He also inspired the whole Cloud computing discussion and the subsequent incubator projects that may result in a financial app store.

- Doc Searls, the open source guru, the wisdom voice of Silicon Valley, and his vendor relationship management idea and inspiration for the Digital Asset Grid (DAG) – see later.

- Craig Burton, one of the fathers of the Internet, and his idea of APIs for future businesses. And his partnership with Doc for the DAG.

- Tony Fish, Kaliya Hamlin – they enlightened, educated and inspired the tribe with everything related to digital identity, digital footprint and slipstream and even digital death.

- Drummond Reed, and his work on the reputation and trust economy.

- Venessa Miemis, and her fresh vision on financial services, her work on Facebook and the future of money, and more generally for keeping us honest.

- Sean Park, for his finance reformation and visioning of the future.

- Antonio (Yobie) Benjamin, and his very powerful demonstration of why the banks are the backbone and need to expose their services through APIs.
- Douglas Rushkoff, and his passionate "program or be programmed" and social currencies discussions.
- Brett King, Shamir Kalkal, Matthias Kroner – the Bank 2.0 guys who shake the tree.
- Mark Pesce, for making us understand hyper-connectivity and for his "by the campfire" incredible summaries.
- Stan Stalnaker, Art Brock, Bernard Lietaer – the complementary, virtual and meta currencies people.
- Jeff Jonas, and his big data ideas and brilliant demonstrations.
- Peter Vander Auwera – of the Innotribe team at SWIFT. The shepherd of this whole tribe, relentlessly devouring incredible amounts of information. Evangelizer of the DAG.
- Matteo Rizzi – of the Innotribe team at SWIFT. The tribe entrepreneur and social media evangelizer.
- Neal Livingston, Dan Marovitz, Kartik Kaushik, Linda McLaughlin-Moore, Gautam Jaim, Andrew Davis, Mircea Mihaescu, John Hagel, Chris Wasden, JP Rangaswami, Laura Merling, Udayan Goyal – the Innotribe Enablers, providing without counting: encouragement, advice, network, friendship.

So if you want to start, get on Google, LinkedIn and start collaborating with one of them.

What's stopping you?

CONCLUSIONS AND RECOMMENDATIONS

Illustration by Mariela Atanassova

CPSIA information can be obtained
at www.ICGtesting.com
Printed in the USA
BVOW05s1124291016
466200BV00010B/949/P